the GODDESS
of HAPPINESS

the GODDESS of HAPPINESS

A Down-to-Earth Guide For Heavenly Balance and Bliss

DEBBIE GISONNI

Inner Ocean Publishing, Inc.
Maui, Hawai'i · San Francisco, California

Inner Ocean Publishing, Inc.
P.O. Box 1239
Makawao, Maui, HI 96768-1239

Cover design by Kathy Wariner
Book design by Maxine Ressler
Author photo by Joe Prestipino

PUBLISHER CATALOGING-IN-PUBLICATION DATA
Gisonni, Debbie.
   The goddess of happiness : a down-to-earth guide for heavenly balance and bliss /
   Debbie Gisonni. — Maui, Hawaii : Inner Ocean, 2005.
      p. ; cm.
      ISBN: 1-930722-48-6
      1. Happiness. 2. Pleasure. 3. Contentment. 4. Women—Psychology. 5. Women—
   Mental health. I. Title.
BF575.H27 G57 2005
158.1—dc22   0504

Printed in the United States of America on recycled paper

05 06 07 08 09 10 DATA 10 9 8 7 6 5 4 3 2 1

Distributed by Publishers Group West

For information on promotions, bulk purchases, premiums, or educational use, please contact
866.731.2216 or sales@innerocean.com.

To Joe and Angela,
who can always make me laugh,
and to Sydney,
who really cracks me up!

"Human happiness transcends
all other worldly considerations."

—ARISTOTLE

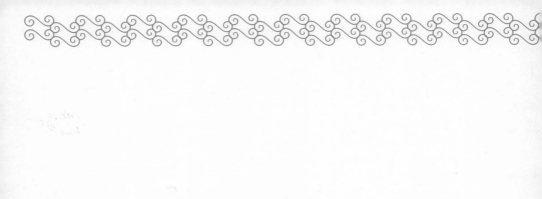

Contents

If I Can Be a Goddess of Happiness, So Can You

THE BULK OF MY CAREER has been spent in the corporate market—specifically, fifteen years in the high-tech industry selling, managing, launching, and publishing computer magazines. While there doesn't seem to be a natural segue between that and *The Goddess of Happiness*, sometimes life takes you down roads you never imagined you'd be traveling on. When I was in the corporate world, I thought I had a perfect life—a lucrative career, a great husband, a home of our own and three dogs (we opted for the four-legged variety of children). I was in control of my destiny . . . or so I thought. As I was climbing the corporate ladder, the family I grew up with started crumbling. One day my mother was dancing the tarantella at an Italian wedding, and the next, she was fighting for her life with a brain tumor that left her permanently disabled. A

couple of years later, my younger sister committed suicide at twenty-three years old. A few months after that, my father was diagnosed with multiple myeloma, a form of bone cancer. Then my favorite aunt, with whom I lived for six months, got breast cancer. All four of them died in a four-year period from 1990 to 1994.

Ironically, 1994 was a milestone year for my career, as I was promoted to the position of publisher. I continued to work incessantly, and as a result, I was rewarded with bigger jobs and more money. It took me another four years to feel the need to make a change, particularly since I wasn't enjoying my work anymore, I had no social life, and I was always sick. In mid-1998, I gave notice and jumped off the corporate treadmill. That decision was immediately followed by a major identity crisis; I spent my free time trying to rediscover who I was outside of my job, and then had to match that person (me, unleashed) with a more meaningful life. After a lot of soul searching, I realized I wasn't the queen bee I once thought I was—instead of being in control of every aspect of my life, I was an ordinary goddess with the power to be happy no matter what path life took me on. I decided to start my own company, Real Life Lessons®, with a mission to help make life easier and happier for women, no matter what challenges they faced. Within two years, my first book, *Vita's Will*, which chronicled my family tragedies and how I survived them, was born.

Somewhere in between shedding my old corporate identity, bearing my soul through my family story, and realizing that no matter what life handed me I had the power within to triumph, I slowly

began surrendering to life as it happened, and a lighter, happier version of me emerged. I became more centered, calm, and knowing, more comfortable being myself, laughing at life, and enjoying every moment of my day. Friends and family members continually tell me, "You look so happy." And I am! Like the phoenix reborn out of the ashes of death, I became the goddess of happiness. No, not the kind of goddess most people imagine, not the mythical Venus or Aphrodite, but a more modern, everyday goddess.

Whether you're dealing with serious tragedy or trivial pursuits, real life for women today is a complicated web of overlapping challenges and responsibilities in work, life, and home. You're racing from one appointment to another—from the office to the gym, from picking up the kids at school to bringing them to soccer practice, from the mall to the doctor's. Your happiness is either last on your "to do" list or nonexistent. Yet isn't happiness the one thing we all want out of life? That's why I created *The Goddess of Happiness: A Down-to-Earth Guide for Heavenly Balance and Bliss*.

I know you don't need another long and complicated "how to" book that you don't have the time and energy to read. So I made this book short and easy to read, with practical nuggets of information you can quickly digest while you're in line at the grocery store and then easily apply to your real life—immediately. You can read this book in one sitting, choose an essay to read at random, and/or use it as a reference when challenges in life arise. Before you begin, I invite you to take the "Are You a Goddess of Happiness?" quiz to help you determine where you are on the happiness scale.

There are forty-four essays in this book, which begs the question: why? Why not a nice round number like forty or fifty? Did I run out of ideas? No, I intentionally chose forty-four because of its meaning in numerology (the ancient science of numbers). Numbers, like colors or words, carry a specific vibration or energy to them, accompanied by distinct traits. In numerology it is common to evaluate the meaning of a number both from the individual digits and from the sum of its digits. The number four denotes a sense of perfect balance and harmony, as in the saying "the four corners of the world." Happiness is dependent upon balance in all areas of your physical and emotional life. The sum of four and four is eight. Eight is the symbol of infinity and abundance in all areas—desiring and receiving the best that life has to offer. Wouldn't that make you happy? And finally, the number forty-four is what is known as a "master number"—one that has a special meaning with unlimited potential. Forty-four is the balance and bridge between the physical and the spiritual. We are spiritual beings living in a physical world—not an easy task, but if you can honor and balance the two, you'll have a thoroughly blissful life by creating heaven on earth!

Each of these forty-four essays ends with five simple ways to achieve an easier and happier life. (Five, by the way, is all about the ability to change and the freedom of new possibilities.) Following the five suggestions is a written affirmation based on the essay topic and an area for you to add your own personal affirmations. Notice the words that appear before the affirmation: *Think it. Say it. Feel it.*

To create happiness in your life, it's important to imagine how it *feels* and really believe it. Writing your affirmations is the first and critical step to setting your intention and ultimately manifesting that which you desire. Your personal affirmations may change over time and should have specific meaning to what is happening in your life. Remember to always state your affirmation in the positive, as if your desire has already come true. Use phrases such as "I am," "I have," "I desire," "I know," "I can," or "I do." Stay away from phrases such as "I hope," "I'll try," or "I want."

As a woman, you are a goddess by default. Yes, it's that simple — no weird rituals, no special clothing, and no physical makeover necessary (although you may find all of that fun). As a goddess, it is your right to stand in your own innate power and claim your happiness. You won't find it by chasing some impossible dream of perfection or by the course of events happening outside of you. Real happiness is found inside of *you*. That's where the goddess is and always has been. Maybe you've never met her or don't believe she exists, but I invite you to find her. Allow this book to reacquaint you with your true self — the goddess of happiness.

Most of all, have fun and enjoy the journey!

Love, light, and laughter,
Debbie Gisonni

Are You a Goddess of Happiness?

1. **When was the last time you laughed out loud?**
    a. Today—you find something to laugh about every day.
    b. A couple of weeks ago you giggled at a friend's joke.
    c. You can't remember laughing in at least a month or more.
2. **When you rise and shine every morning, are you:**
    a. Ready to embrace what the day will bring.
    b. Sometimes wishing you were doing something else.
    c. Dreading the thought of what lies ahead.
3. **A girlfriend has called and invited you to the latest "chick flick," but you have too much to do. Do you:**
    a. Ditch your "to do" list for another day and go to the movie to laugh and cry.
    b. Take a rain check so you can finish your work.
    c. Say yes, but frantically try to finish your tasks before you leave.
4. **A typical day in the life of _____(your name here) is:**
    a. The perfect combination of work and play.
    b. Exhausting, yet you still get a little downtime.
    c. Like doing the Indy 500 without any pit stops.
5. **When you look in the mirror, what do you see?**

a. A confident and beautiful goddess looking back at you.

b. An everyday woman with her good days and bad.

c. Nothing—you avoid mirrors at all costs.

6. **You're having an operation, and you'll be on crutches for two weeks. Needing some extra help around the house, do you:**

a. Ask a friend or family member for help or suggestions.

b. Hire a crew of professionals to come in.

c. Tough it out on your own.

7. **When was the last time you pampered yourself?**

a. You just did! That last massage is still fresh on your mind.

b. Not for a few months and only on special occasions.

c. Too long ago to remember—who has time for that?

8. **You've come down with a mild case of the flu. You immediately think:**

a. "It's a good thing it was just a mild case—I'll be over it in no time."

b. "I wish I didn't get sick this week."

c. "I always get sick!"

9. **What do you think about spending time alone?**

a. You savor every moment and make it a priority in your life.

b. You take the time whenever you can, which isn't often.

c. You never have time alone and wouldn't know what to do if you did.

10. **What does being a goddess mean to you?**

a. You! A fun, vivacious, confident, strong, and intuitive woman.

b. Definitely not you, but you have some friends who would qualify.

c. You're not sure you believe in real-life goddesses.

If you chose mostly A's:

Congratulations! You *are* a goddess of happiness! You have a zest for life, and always see the glass half-full. You're the woman who lights up a room when you enter and whose attention everyone wants. You genuinely love and respect yourself and others, and don't mind showing it off with your cool confidence and generous heart. Inside and out, you're the goddess you want to be. Pampering yourself with a day off or a soothing massage nurtures your spirit. Goddess, keep shining your light wherever you go and remember to spread your infectious laugh to others as well. When you share your secrets of joy with friends and family, you become the supreme goddess of happiness.

If you chose mostly B's:

Good going! You are almost ready to pull off that last veil of "serious thinking" for a life filled with daily fun and happy dreams. Yes, it *is* possible! It's all just waiting for you to say, "Yes, I want it!" You already have a good appreciation of life and positive opinion of who you are—just take it to the next level, goddess. Make yourself and your happiness number one in your life. Sure, you can still keep nurturing those around you, which you love to do, but leave some precious time to feed your own mind, body, and spirit. What is it that you love to do . . . sailing, reading, dancing? Do more of it, and there will be no turning back. You'll become a goddess of happiness before you can say, "Another chocolate? Of course!"

If you chose mostly C's:

Get started! The goddess of happiness in you is collecting all-too-serious dust. She's yearning to get cleaned up and come out and play. Dig down deep into your inner well of happiness and you'll find her there, waiting for you. Yes, she *is* there! The inner goddess is like a bellybutton: everyone has one, although some may not be so obvious as others. Try not to take life so seriously—it's not brain surgery. Play hooky once in awhile from work and daily responsibilities, jump in a rain puddle, take a pottery class, go out with friends. Lighten up and laugh more often. All this fun will help you find and nurture the goddess inside you, and soon you'll be dusting her off and showing the world the new you—a goddess of happiness.

I

Be the Goddess You Are

Do you sometimes feel as if the true woman you are is locked up in a closet collecting dust along with those low-cut jeans you'll never have the courage to wear? Do you hide parts of yourself in order to please someone else? If the package you present to the world is a neatly wrapped, square blue box when you're really a yellow-and-purple drawstring velvet bag with fringe on the bottom, you are living a lie. Covering up essential parts of yourself (and I don't mean a sarong over a bathing suit) will eventually block out your true essence—the goddess within you.

When we think of modern-day goddesses, our attention naturally goes toward top female celebrities such as Madonna or Cher—beautiful, talented, successful, and sassy. Women who can push the emotional buttons of society with the way they dress or act. Women who are not afraid to speak their mind, even if others don't agree. Women who can run a business empire and also be a star, a mother,

and a lover at the same time. But what about the rest of us—the everyday women living everyday lives?

There are everyday women—you know who they are—who light up a room whenever they enter. People naturally gravitate to them, like mosquitoes circling a patio lamp. These women are usually not the prettiest or the smartest or the thinnest, but there's something about them that shines. You can't quite pinpoint what it is, but you know you want some of it. Well, guess what? You can't have it because what they have is unique to them. All they've done is be the goddess they really are inside. You can't be *that* goddess, but you can be your own goddess. *You* are the only person in charge of your own inner light. It's your choice to turn it on or off.

I know that at first you might not consider yourself a goddess, but what if I told you that you are. Anytime I meet someone new, I start to see her as a goddess. I notice how her facial features, which might have seemed ordinary at first, fit her persona like a snug glove. Her other attributes—such as the way she moves her body, the sound of her voice, and the texture of her hair—all paint a unique picture that is a reflection of her spirit inside. As I spend more time with her, observing and appreciating her qualities, I can't imagine her wanting to be anything other than what she is—a loving, giving, perfect creature—a goddess.

Rediscover yourself—your true self. Maybe you'll awaken your fiery side, like the Hawaiian volcano goddess Pele, or your mothering instincts, like the ancient Greek goddess Demeter. Whatever

you find, dust it off and shine it up. Bring forth the true light within you, which no one can ever duplicate or take away. Dare to be who you really are and dare to experience life in full color!

Five Ways to Be the Goddess You Are:

* Make a collage of all the things that represent who you are — keep it handy for reference.

* Say what you mean and mean what you say.

* Create your own look (hair, face, clothes) that is pleasing to you.

* Always act with integrity, in every situation and with every person.

* Accentuate your unique personality or physical traits.

> ### Think it. Say it. Feel it.
> *I know and honor my true self and allow it to shine with others.*

My personal affirmations to be the goddess I am:

....

....

....

....

....

2

Be Present

HAVE YOU EVER watched what dogs do most of the day? Basically, they lie around doing nothing. I'm always curious to know what they're thinking about, or if they're thinking at all. Judging by my dogs, I'm sure their thoughts have something to do with their next meal, massage, or walk. We humans tend to spend a lot of time thinking, particularly women who are masters at multitasking. How many uniquely different things can you be thinking of at one time? What to make for dinner, your child's parent-teacher conference, the dog's vet appointment, a deadline at work, the paint colors for the new bathroom? Scary, huh? We think about what has already happened or what we assume might happen much more so than what is happening right now. All this time spent in the past and future leaves little or no time for the present, which is the only time that matters.

It seems that something always has to go wrong in order to force us to stop and be present. For example, when you have to drive your

car through a heavy snowstorm, you can't help but pay attention to every bump and slide. Normally, though, you're driving in auto-pilot while your mind is working overtime: "How late will this traffic make me? I need to pick up Emily from her soccer game. What am I making for dinner tonight?"

I have a beautiful, kind, loving, and generous friend who seems to spend her whole life racing. In the twenty years since I've known her, she's always running late from one appointment to the next, talking a mile a minute and putting out some sort of emotional fire at the same time. Sometimes when I'm with her, I feel as if I'm in one of those zany dreams where you keep jumping from one unrelated scene to another, with no beginning and no end—just continuous but different streams of consciousness. Meanwhile, I'm gripping the bottom of my seat with sweat-drenched hands and wondering if she's going to step on the brake before crashing into the car stopped in front of us. It's not that I think she's a bad driver. In fact, she's never had any accidents with me in the car (I can't speak for anyone else). It's just that I know she's not present. I'm sure her inner goddess is constantly crying out, "Stop, look, and listen now," and while she might have heard this amid the clutter of her mind, she's already deleted that scene and moved on to a few others.

There will be times in your life where you rush to get to the next thing—your job, your appointments, your partner, your house—without any consideration or participation in the current thing, whatever that might be. When you look back, life all becomes one

big blur of images, like sticking your head out the window of a speeding car. You're unable to clearly see anything, whether it's right next to you, in front, or behind.

Life is in its most perfect state when you are present in every moment. Living in the past or future, as we often do, only serves to drain your spirit. You can't change what has happened, nor can you worry about what hasn't happened yet. So instead of living in the land of "I could've, should've, would've" or "what if," try living in the land of "I am," because *now* is the only moment a goddess can affect and enjoy.

As poet Elizabeth Barrett Browning said, "Light tomorrow with today!"

Five Ways to Be Present:

* Stop and notice every detail in the backdrop of your daily life—the colors, smells, and people.

* Savor each moment in life. Like snowflakes, no two are the same.

* Good or bad, keep the past in the past and live in the "now."

* Stop worrying about what you can't change or don't know.

* Concentrate on one thing—whatever you're doing or saying at this very moment.

Think it. Say it. Feel it.

I think, speak, act and live in the present moment.

My personal affirmations to be present:

....

....

....

....

....

3

Choose Joy

WHAT IS JOY to you? It can certainly take many forms. For one woman, it may be the sound of children laughing or the smell of puppy breath. For another, it's dancing in the moonlight or eating ice cream. For yet another, it could be a soothing massage or pedicure.

We often associate joy with the things and events in our lives that produce the warmest and fuzziest feelings of pleasure, but true joy requires no external stimuli. It's a state of mind that exists regardless of what's happening around you. Children can easily find laughter and joy in just being. I once read that children laugh hundreds of times a day. Goldie Hawn, who seems to have a perpetual giggling child inside of her, once said in an interview that all she ever wanted to be when she grew up was happy—just like she was as a kid. As an adult, she makes a conscious effort to pursue inner happiness through quiet meditation. Her inside joy is reflected in her outside life and work, including a documentary she developed called *In Search of Joy* and an organization she founded, the Bright

Light Foundation, to help young people live more positive and fulfilling lives.

Bringing joy to others feeds our own happiness. If you grew up around my family, you'd know that food always brought us much joy—preparing it, serving it, eating it, or just talking about it. I remember a story my father used to tell me about a time when he was away from home in the Marines. One day, a package arrived from his mother containing a homemade blueberry pie. He was so excited that he and his comrades skipped the utensils, broke through the flaky crust with their hands, and shoveled the gooey mixture into their watering mouths. There was a look of sheer joy in my father's eyes each time he told that story. Later in his life, when he was dying of bone cancer, I personally carried a homemade blueberry pie on a plane from California to New York, just to see his face light up one last time. Even when people are dying, you can bring a little joy into their lives . . . and yours.

Joy can be accessed during both the happiest and most difficult times in your life, because it is present in your heart at all times. You have a place for it inside of you (which can be found) and a memory of it (which can be reproduced). Reaching into your store of joy is like going to the automatic teller machine and making a withdrawal of happiness. But unlike your bank account, there's an unlimited supply of joy to receive and share!

Abraham Lincoln said, "Most people are about as happy as they choose to be." As a goddess, it's your choice to use your joy, and your privilege to share it.

Five Ways to Choose Joy:

* Recall a happy memory and focus on it long enough to bring back the feeling.

* Laugh, smile, and joke whenever and wherever you can.

* Call or see an upbeat girlfriend.

* Take a break from TV news and violent shows and watch a romantic comedy.

* Avoid negative or angry people.

Think it. Say it. Feel it.

My life is full of joy, and I share that joy with others.

My personal affirmations to choose joy:

....

....

....

....

....

4

Give Up Control

I've hated surprise parties ever since my mother threw me one for my sixteenth birthday—an age when the last thing you want to do is party with your mother and her friends. I never encourage visitors to drop by my house without calling first. And I would never allow the success of a dinner party I'm giving to be contingent upon what guests bring . . . or don't. Call me a control freak (I prefer to use the term "Type A personality"), but I like things to run smoothly and as planned. I can't help it. I was born Type A, all the way—driven to succeed, no matter what the challenge. Organized, productive, and reliable. Always in control. For that, I received much praise and acceptance from my family, friends, teachers, and business colleagues. All of this adoration, of course, only encouraged me to become even *more* efficient. How great to be in complete control of my own destiny! Whether it was the next job I wanted or my next day's outfit, I planned and executed each with the same intensity and drive. Like a hungry cheetah chasing a gazelle, there was nothing stopping me in my run from point A to point B.

Then life threw me a couple of unexpected curves, all outside of my control. That sense of security and control I had built my life upon was instantly proven nonexistent—a mirage between my mind and reality. It took awhile for me to figure out that there are scenes on this grand stage of life that are impromptu and uncontrollable. During those times, the only healthy thing to do is to give up control, and surrender.

My friend Lisa worked long hours as a software programmer. When her employer downsized the workforce, her workload increased to compensate for the people who were let go. She began having chronic pain in her neck and arms but continued to work at a frenzied pace for another year until numbness prevented her from doing her job. Reluctantly, she left her job on disability. After reevaluating her career and her life, she decided to go back to school for a different degree and start a new career.

Surrendering does not mean giving up your power. It's more about asking the universe to come to your aid and trusting that it will. Yemaya is the ancient African goddess of surrender, also known as the goddess of the ocean. Legend says she effortlessly gave birth to fourteen spirits in the water by surrendering to divine will and thus allowing what was to happen to happen naturally. (Spirits must obviously come out of the womb easier than babies!)

If you're like me, maybe you need to hit a brick wall (or two) before you finally surrender that gripping hold you have on every outcome in your life. When my will is bruised and battered, I naturally loosen up the reigns of control, mainly because I have no energy left to fight. If you're set on a particular goal and can only see one path to get there, you're cheating yourself of happiness that can come in unexpected ways. You become a six-foot, five-inch brawny bouncer blocking the front door of a nightclub called "Unlimited Possibilities." You always have the option to move away from the door and see what comes in and out. If you choose not to exercise that option, you may end up getting trampled in the battle between your will and your life.

It is only when you surrender control of your life and of the lives of others that you truly become an empowered goddess. That's when you can believe in miracles, and dreams that come true with just a wish, not a plan.

Five Ways to Give Up Control:

* Consider unexpected change to be an opportunity to learn and a gift to grow.

* Be open to multiple ways of reaching a goal, even those you haven't thought of yet.

* Believe that everything happens for a reason, even if you don't know why—just let it be.

* Take a day off from lists and plans and see what happens; go with the flow.

* Give up controlling the way other people live their lives, even if you think they should do it differently.

> **Think it. Say it. Feel it.**
>
> *I surrender my expectations of people and situations.*

My personal affirmations to give up control:

....

....

....

....

....

5

Stop the Noise

Do you remember those lazy summer vacation mornings when you were a kid? I used to stay in bed after waking up and just stare at the ceiling, listening to nothing. As the rising sun splashed on my bedroom walls, I felt so peaceful and happy lying in bed, soaking up the silence. It was the only time during the day when my mind wasn't cluttered with the noises of the external world.

For most women, those quiet summer mornings have been long forgotten and replaced with the never-ending morning noise of phones ringing, kids screaming, dogs barking, and TV blasting. Being still, even for a moment, seems totally unnecessary and, even more so, detrimental to the constantly moving treadmill of life we run upon as if we'll lose our place in life if we stop. In our techno-logically advanced culture, filled with stimuli to keep us going twenty-four hours a day, there is no encouragement for silence or reflection—unless you're a three-year-old child in time-out! Most

of us shun silence, opting instead to spend whatever time we have alone drowning in the constant din of the TV.

While I was in between careers, I spent a lot of time doing nothing, which led to an interest in meditating—in essence, the same thing as doing nothing. Yes, me . . . the person who used to wake up in the middle of the night to add to my "to do" list for the next day. Once I started meditating, however, I found I wasn't as anxious at night and was able to rekindle the feelings from those peaceful quiet childhood summer mornings at any time. And, in the silence of meditation, I hear the most profound things.

But don't take my word for it. Technology (it does good things, too) can now prove the actual benefits of meditation. Advanced brain-scan imaging has shown that meditation can rewire the neurons in the brain, with numerous life-improving benefits—it can help boost the immune system, reduce stress, extend life, slow disease, manage pain, and alleviate depression . . . to name a few.

You can find silence anywhere—in a raging crowd or a quiet forest. It's not about what's going on outside of you—it's what you create inside. In as little as ten minutes you can become the calm in the center of a hurricane that's whirling around you. Start with a few deep goddess breaths. The Buddhist spiritual leader Thich Nhat Hanh suggests a breathing technique to help quiet your mind. While taking a breath in, say to yourself, "Breathing in, I am aware of breathing in." As you release the breath, say, "Breathing out, I am aware of breathing out." All you need is a little practice and

commitment, and you'll be well on your way to having a more peaceful goddess existence.

Five Ways to Stop the Noise:

* Join a weekly meditation group, or start one on your own.

* Create a ten-minute daily ritual (upon waking or before sleep) for prayer, meditation, or silence.

* Turn on the TV only to watch something you really want to see—not for background noise while you're busy doing other things.

* Take a walk in nature.

* Practice doing absolutely nothing.

Think it. Say it. Feel it.

I am able to go to a quiet place inside of me . . . anytime, anywhere.

My personal affirmations to stop the noise:

....

....

....

....

....

6

Honor Freedom

JUST SAYING THE word "freedom" stirs up all kinds of emotions in women, from euphoria to anger to sadness. Freedom and human rights for women have been challenged or abused from the beginning of time as we know it. The abusers, whether political parties, religious institutions, or individuals, were usually on one mission: to gain control, power, or money. Horrific crimes against women are still going on today around the world, from Chinese baby girls being killed to Middle Eastern women being routinely raped or sexually mutilated. A report issued by the United Nations Development Fund for Women found that one in three women globally is likely to be raped, beaten, or otherwise abused in her lifetime. All of this seems so far away, but we need only look out our own back doors to witness the freedom of women and girls being challenged every day, right here in America. Bullies in the schoolyards, sexual harassment in the workplace, crimes of hate, protests against

gay marriages — these and countless more offenses chip away at freedom like a gold miner's ax prying apart the most precious and shiniest pieces of a woman's essence.

What business is it of anyone's (male or female) to tell a woman what choices to make in her life — religious, sexual, or otherwise? Think how much easier and less frustrating life would be if we stopped wasting all that time trying to dictate how others should live. As long as someone is not harming another person, why can't we let her worship whomever she wants, love whomever she wants, and be whoever she wants to be? After centuries of suppression, we women should be entitled to make our own choices and exercise our own free will. We should also extend that freedom of choice to others as well.

You are a goddess with a free spirit and the right to choose your own beliefs, habits, and affiliations. Countless women in history have fought for your rights. Susan B. Anthony is recognized mainly for her role in giving women the right to vote, but she also spoke out against slavery, worked as an advocate for women and children who suffered from alcoholic husbands, and fought for equal pay for women. It's easy to take these rights for granted when you haven't fought the battle yourself. It's the difference between making an apple pie from scratch (growing the apples, picking them, and kneading the dough) and walking into a store and buying it ready-made. But it wasn't so long ago that women didn't have the luxury of the latter approach. After all, it was only about 150 years ago that Emma Snodgrass was arrested in Boston for wearing pants!

Remember to exercise your freedom every day—get involved, speak up, stand up for your rights, vote—and support that freedom for women around the world. Life is a wonderful thing—ask anyone who is dying. Freedom in life is even more wonderful—ask anyone who doesn't have it.

Five Ways to Honor Freedom:

* Support women's rights in your own neighborhood and around the world (through making donations, starting petitions, and lobbying our politicians).

* Instill confidence, power, and equality in your daughters and all young girls.

* Speak up if you see anyone's rights, including your own, being violated.

* Learn about the challenges and atrocities women face all over the world—use this knowledge to appreciate your own freedom or to get involved on a larger scale.

* Give others in your life the same freedom of choice that you enjoy every day.

Think it. Say it. Feel it.

I have freedom of choice in my life and support the same freedom in the lives of all women.

My personal affirmations to honor freedom:

....

....

....

....

....

7

Celebrate Diversity

AMERICANS OFTEN TAKE pride in the fact that we have a diverse population consisting of different races, religions, and nationalities. One would assume an environment such as this would encourage and celebrate the differences among us. Why, then, does our multicultural society often make us feel ashamed to be different?

Aside from my looks (olive skin, dark hair), much of my ethnicity growing up was defined by the food I ate. As a child in grade school, I remember being singled out and embarrassed by classmates for the lunch my Italian immigrant mother used to pack for me. Crushed meatballs or pepper and onion frittata stuffed into a thick hunk of Italian bread gave a whole new meaning to the brown-bag lunch. Once I opened the olive oil–stained bag, the smell of garlic and onions permeated the entire lunch room! Inevitably, someone would ask me, "What is *that?*" The tone of those three little words made me yearn for a plain bologna or peanut butter

and jelly sandwich on white bread! Today I appreciate all that sumptuous ethnic food, not only for the taste, but for the fact that it was the cornerstone of my family's cultural rituals—the 1 P.M. Sunday afternoon mandatory pasta meal, the 6 A.M. aroma of garlic and onions simmering in olive oil, the sizzling roast leg of lamb (not turkey!) on holidays.

I don't believe America is as much of a melting pot as it is a nation of people with unique differences—some of which have been borrowed from each other and assimilated into the American culture. Funny how we are so quick to demand diversity in everything we consume—from the food we eat to the flowers we plant to the cars we buy—yet when it comes to the category of people, we want everyone to be the same. What an absurd and boring concept! We all come into this world with our own special qualities—the color of our skin, the food we eat, our sexual preferences, religious beliefs, and personalities. No one should ever be left out, embarrassed, or, even worse, killed for being different. In a *MORE* magazine article, Vanessa Williams, America's first African American Miss America winner in 1983 (minorities were prohibited to enter the pageant until the fifties), spoke of receiving hate letters and death threats from the Ku Klux Klan for her participation in the contest. On the other hand, members of her own race weren't pleased with her as well. They accused her of not being "black enough"!

Children quickly learn to practice prejudice from their parents and friends, but they can just as easily be taught how wrong it is.

Imagine what your school years might have been like if all the kids accepted each other's differences. No fights, no bullies, no embarrassment. Now think of that concept on a broader scale. What would happen if we required the families of people at war to spend a week living together, learning about each other, and peacefully exchanging cultural rituals, food, and conversation? Maybe they would figure out how much more alike than different they are, because they share the most common bond there is—that of being part of the human race!

Have you ever heard of the Black Madonna? No, she isn't a pop star, but she does have millions of devotees around the world. Her origins are mysterious yet ubiquitous. Some say she is the ancient earth goddess who was later converted to the fair-skinned Mary by Christianity. Other evidence places her as Isis in ancient Egyptian times, over 300 years before the first dynasty, with later adaptations by the Greeks as Demeter and the Romans as Ceres. She has been called Venus, Kali, Diana, and Mary Magdalene. Are they all one and the same? Maybe. Maybe she is a reminder of the blending of all human kind, as no single group can claim her as their own—she belongs to everyone.

Five Ways to Celebrate Diversity:

* Take time to learn about and appreciate different cultures through books, documentaries, magazines, travel, foreign language classes, or cooking classes.

* When you meet people who are different from you, welcome them into your circle, ask them about their culture, and be open to talking about yours.

* Teach your children not to judge people by what they look like.

* Don't form opinions of nations of people only by what the news media reports.

* Plan a monthly trip to your nearest big city, even if it's just to walk around.

Think it. Say it. Feel it.

I see differences among people as unique and special gifts to humanity.

My personal affirmations to celebrate diversity:

....

....

....

....

....

8

Participate in Your Life

IF LIFE WERE a pair of DKNY jeans, what would yours look like? Would they be worn and faded, thinning in spots, soft to the touch with the hem unraveling? Or would they be crisp and clean with perfect creases and the tags still on them? If my mother had her way, mine would be the latter. I was raised with what I call a "life-saver" mentality. No, not the candy but the kind of environment where couch cushions were covered in plastic and never touched by human flesh, where bathroom towels were only for show or company, where money was saved and only spent on necessities, where new clothes were never worn right after you bought them, where entire rooms in the house were not used, and where the only lit candles were on birthday cakes or in church.

Many women in my mother's generation saved *and* collected a lot of things they never used. Nothing too expensive—maybe a series of decorative plates you see on late-night TV or a porcelain doll

advertised in *Reader's Digest*, complete with the birth certificate. When my aunt died, we found dozens of limited-edition plates depicting everything from Elvis movie scenes to Chinese children playing—all in their original boxes with protective coverings and sales receipts, tucked away in drawers and closets, never displayed, never used, never enjoyed. Why spend the money just to hide them?

Too often we save things in life for the wrong reasons. Besides material goods, we save our emotions because we don't want to be hurt, our appearance because we don't want to look old, or our flaws because we don't want to be anything less than the perfect woman. All this saving prevents us from fully participating in the journey of life. We become bystanders watching our lives go by instead of participating in new experiences.

Today, make a point of lighting all the candles in your house and allowing them to burn instead of collecting dust. Although some prefer to stoke a log or two in the fireplace, I prefer to line up about a dozen candles in my fireplace—all different sizes, colors, fragrances, and shapes—and light them while becoming mesmerized by the dancing flames that look as if they're playing a well-orchestrated piece of silent music. Just like the unique direction each life takes, and the variety of experiences that await us, no two candles melt the same way—some drip slowly like sap on a tree; some widen their walls like the mouth of a·cave, exposing their shimmering light; and some collapse inward, engulfing their flame like molten lava. You'll never know how yours will burn unless you light it. A half-melted candle is like a wise middle-aged woman who has enjoyed and savored life — a goddess who is not afraid to continue to ignite the flame of life until there is nothing left but a tiny piece of metal that once held the cord to that life's existence.

Allow the flame of life to entrance you, burn you, titillate your senses, soften you. Participate in life and you'll have more fun than you ever imagined!

Five Ways to Participate in Your Life:

* When you have a rainy day, use what you saved for it.

* Don't hold back your feelings, especially those of love and compassion.

* Try something new — a sport, an adventure, love, a hat, or a hairstyle.

* Once in awhile, jump up and down on the bed with your kids (or even by yourself).

* Use and share your belongings; you can't take them with you when you're gone.

Think it. Say it. Feel it.

I choose to participate in all that is available to me in every moment of every day.

My personal affirmations to participate in my life:

....

....

....

....

....

9

Think Positively

Have you ever wondered where the expression "knock on wood" comes from? There are several theories dating back to the Pagans, Christians, and ancient Celtics. The most common is that knocking on a tree woke the good spirits who would protect people from evil. Today's version includes knocking on any wood-like surface, but the premise remains the same—you knock on wood to prevent bad luck. To me, "knock on wood" is a form of negative thinking—it's focusing on the bad (that terrible thing that could happen) instead of the good.

You bring into your life that which you focus upon. If you're one of those women who thrives on gloom and doom, yanking others into your web of despair and then gloating about your foresight when life becomes as miserable as you feared—guess what? That behavior creates your own self-fulfilling prophecy! You will always live in victim mode, shunning happiness while you anticipate your next inevitable misfortune.

Amid these forces of negativity, notice that there are other goddesses who always seem cheerful and who are able to find the good in any situation or person. The words "Murphy's law" never touch their lips! You may think that they have all the good luck. And they do! Because they focus on how great things are or can be, versus what can ruin their happiness. And, if something does go wrong, they find the lesson in the experience—maybe even the silver lining—and move on positively. These are the people who choose optimism and think positively.

When I woke up one day to find my car tire flat in my driveway, I didn't think, "These things always happen to me." Instead I chose to think, "Wasn't I lucky to have this happen here, instead of while I was driving sixty miles an hour on the freeway?" Okay . . . you say, "Big deal! It's just a flat tire. What about the really bad stuff that happens to us?"

Martha Washington said, "The greater part of our happiness or misery depends on our dispositions and not on our circumstances." Katie Couric (the very cutest girl next door with the ear-to-ear smile on her face on network TV news) lost her husband and the father of her two children to colon cancer in 1998. While she admits to going through a very angry period, she's an optimist by nature. After her loss, she decided to help educate the public about colon cancer—first by having her own colonoscopy in front of millions of people on live TV, and then by continuing her commitment as a spokesperson for the disease. Colonoscopy test rates have increased by 20 percent since then. In a *Reader's Digest* interview, when asked whether she feels that she's had more than her share of hardship, Katie replied, "No. There are plenty of people who have had more sadness in their lives than I have." Katie made a conscious choice to turn a personal tragedy into something positive for herself and others.

While Katie Couric may have just been born optimistic, a positive attitude can be learned at any age. If no one in your life was a role model on how to be positive, then it becomes your duty to learn. You create the reality around you with your thoughts, words, and actions. It's the law of the universe: What you put out, you get back. Simple. Negativity zaps so much energy from you and ends up coming back ten times stronger. It's cold, dark, and heavy on your soul. Being cheerful and optimistic, however, feels like a cool summer breeze—light, sweet, and airy. Try it sometime; you may never go back.

Five Ways to Think Positively:

* Hang around positive people even if it seems uncomfortable at first.

* If you work or live with negative people, don't get pulled into their fear or allow them to impose their opinions upon you.

* Practice changing every negative thought and word to a positive one.

* Always assume the best from people and situations.

* Make positive affirmations—if you say it enough, you'll start believing it.

Think it. Say it. Feel it.
I can easily find the positive side of every situation.

My personal affirmations to think positively:

....

....

....

....

....

IO

Indulge

Indulgences come in many forms—cleaning services, massage therapists, hair colorists, gardeners, or even a quiet bath. Ironically, the indulgence that women are always meant to feel horrible about is one that was not only permitted but encouraged in my family—eating your favorite foods. In an Italian household, food equaled life, comfort, and happiness. Given today's obsession with dieting and the ultra-thin body, the consumption of one chocolate caramel could send a goddess packing for a week-long guilt trip. If I see one more ad about a "low-carb" food, I'll gag. "Low carb" today is like "low sugar" in the nineties or "low fat" in the eighties—pick your craze and the media will eat it up, so to speak. Yes, I do understand the health risks of being overweight and under exercised, and I don't condone poor eating habits or couch potatoes, but I do believe that excessive restrictions only lead to more problems. Moderation in eating is the key. Sometimes denying yourself that one special treat can result in a major food binge later on.

Another way I choose to indulge myself is spending time with my goddess friends—a totally delightful treat for me. Some women have a difficult time making this a priority in their lives, mainly because they feel guilty if they don't spend all their free time with their husbands, partners, or children. While the role of the nurturer is a commendable one, if you don't nurture yourself, what have you got left to give to others? Getting out a bit on your own will make you a better mother or lover. Some of my friends' husbands have a hard time when their wives go out with girlfriends. The husbands feel rejected and abandoned and frequently try to make my friends feel guilty for having any fun without them. Needless to say, these couples have been in and out of therapy.

It's perfectly okay to indulge as long as you're not hurting yourself or another person. And never allow yourself to feel guilty about it afterward, as the guilt negates all the enjoyment you received, which was the objective in the first place. Life *should* be enjoyable. If we constantly deny ourselves that which feeds our body, mind, and spirit, we can never be happy. Indulgences give you something to look forward to after a long day or difficult week. Like a personal mini-vacation, an indulgence offers you a quick mental health break by allowing you to do something that makes you feel good. Famous chef Julia Child said, "Life itself is the proper binge."

Sometimes you just need to have your cake and eat it too. And . . . don't forget the ice cream!

Five Ways to Indulge:

* When receiving a service such as a massage, focus on the pleasure of it rather than on your "to do" list.

* Within your budget, hire people to do chores if it allows you more quality time with your family and friends.

* If you must have something that's not on your diet and it won't cause you physical harm, eat it and enjoy every bite. Go back on the diet the next day, guilt-free!

* If you have children, trade babysitting time with other mothers so you have time alone or with your partner.

* Always indulge in moderation, or the indulgence will lose its special feeling.

Think it. Say it. Feel it.
I cheerfully feed my passions and my soul.

My personal affirmations to indulge:

II

Let Passion Flow

HAVE YOU EVER watched musicians perform? I'm not talking about just listening, but really watching their body movements and facial expressions. Once I saw a Santana concert on TV. I've always loved their music, but on that evening, as the camera cut to each band member's solo, I was watching rather than listening. I started to notice how their personas transformed while they were singing, drumming, or playing the guitar. Their faces contorted to the beat of the music, heads cocked from one side to the other, eyes closed—looking within. What I saw for the first time was how much passion Carlos Santana and his band members had for their music. It was as if they *became* the music. They were no longer performers on stage; they were music and soul, joined as one.

When my husband, Joe, decided to give up his eighteen-year career in high tech, he considered photography (a lifelong interest) as a new venture, but his logical mind didn't feel at ease with it. So I asked him some questions: "How do you feel when you walk into

a camera store and see all that equipment and beautiful photography displayed? Do you feel like a kid in a candy store? Do you love the smell of it? Do you want to stay forever? Do you even get a little excited?" His answer—"Yes! Yes! Yes to all of it!" Okay, maybe he didn't admit to getting excited, but photography was his passion, and to be true to himself, he needed to pursue it.

You can always tell if a person is passionate about something just by listening and watching her talk about it. Her face lights up and her eyes twinkle, as if there's a current of electricity swirling inside her. Think of TV personality Nigella Lawson as she licks cake batter off her fingers. You can almost taste the chocolate as you watch her gobbling it up and smacking her lips. Or think of author Frances Mayes talking about her adventures in Italy. Her descriptions will make you want to buy a villa in Tuscany and pick olives the rest of your life. The passion of these women for what they love makes them sensual, inviting, and interesting goddesses. When you see them, you think, "I want some of what she has—that energy . . . that joy." You *can* have it.

Passion is the feeling that comes from deep within your heart; it's a bubbling cauldron of hot liquid. You can try to put a lid on it, but the steam escapes every now and then, reminding you of what is just beneath the surface, feeding your soul. Most of us have a passion for something in life. Maybe it's spending time with your children, skiing, or watching old movies. It's what gives you joy. It's what brings a smile to your face. It's what allows you the freedom of creativity without the burden of logic.

Being passionate is a true sign of embracing the spirit of the goddess within. Find your passion and make it a part of who you are. When you unleash your passion in life, even the most mundane or stressful moments of your day become easier to handle.

Five Ways to Let Passion Flow:

* Notice what makes your heart flutter, and do more of it.

* Send loving thoughts to every task, person, or situation.

* At least once a week, do something you love for an hour.

* Join a group with similar interests as yours.

* Share your passion. (If it's knitting, give away knitted gifts. If it's cooking, bring a dish to a friend's party.)

Think it. Say it. Feel it.
I find and express my passion for people and experiences that move me.

My personal affirmations to let passion flow:

....
....
....
....
....

12

Open Your Mind and Heart

Ask any mother what she wants most of all for her children, and she's likely to say, "I just want them to be happy." Yet the things that make some teens happy these days (multiple piercings, purple hair, black lipstick) are probably not what their mothers had in mind. My friend Kim's sixteen-year-old son, Drew, wanted to get a tattoo for years—nothing outlandish or satanic—just a drawing of a sun on his shoulder. After much deliberation, Kim decided he could get it. Drew was a good kid, and Kim felt that if she had to pick her battles, she'd rather win the more important ones such as those involving drugs or smoking. The tattoo could be covered with a shirt and was perfectly legal with parental consent. And, since she gave Drew plenty of time for the novelty of the idea to wear off and he still wanted the tattoo, she knew it wasn't just a passing fancy. Every generation of teens has its idiosyncrasies that make them unique *and* help them fit in at the same time.

Teens aren't the only ones who require us to look beyond our com-

fort zone in life. People of all ages need to be understanding with each other as well. If a girlfriend or family member wants to do something you think is ridiculous, don't form an immediate negative judgment. As long as what they want to do is not against the law, doesn't physically harm the person or others, and isn't an act of prejudice or violence, open your heart and mind to the person's motivations, desires, and points of reference. Asking questions will help.

Teachers are called upon to have tremendous understanding for children who aren't their own and whom they may only know for one school season. One of my childhood friends became a special-education teacher. Her "kids," as she calls them, face socioeconomic as well as mental challenges. No matter what profanity they yell or violent outburst they have, Diane says she loves teaching them every day. Having an understanding of the challenges they confront at home, in life, and in their own heads helps her to see beyond the surface of their actions. Eleanor Roosevelt said, "Understanding is a two-way street." If you take the time to learn more about the subject and engage the other person, you'll naturally be more educated and tolerant. After all, "to understand" means to have learned.

Five Ways to Open Your Mind and Heart:

* When your child wants something you disapprove of, remember how you felt at that age and try to understand her needs.

* Support your friends' and family's choices in their lives, even if they seem outrageous to you.

* Before making a negative judgment, talk it over with others and research the topic.

* Respect that each person has free will and needs to express herself in ways that may only make sense to her.

* Life is a series of compromises—avoid the attitude that it's your way or no way.

Think it. Say it. Feel it.

I easily understand people and events, without judgment.

My personal affirmations to open my mind and heart:

....

....

....

....

....

13

Eat Humble Pie

"ENOUGH ABOUT YOU, let's get to me!" How many times have you heard that tune playing in your own head? Being in front, first, and recognized is highly encouraged in our society. We place more value on humiliation than humility, because we think that standing out is better than staying within. Just watch a few minutes of any reality show, and you'll see how easily people volunteer to endure public humiliation for fifteen minutes of fame. Oh . . . those poor bachelorettes who get that single rose *and* the boot!

Between my first and second book, I had a rough time—emotionally, physically, and financially. I had yet to be recognized nationally for my work (Oprah wasn't calling!), my husband was in between careers, and a back injury prevented me from writing. One day I was caught in a traffic jam on my way to an appointment in San Francisco. I got increasingly frustrated sitting there, as my mind started replaying all my problems. By the time I arrived in the city,

I was depressed about my career and my life. I kept thinking about poor little me.

As I drove through the city, I saw the familiar sight of street beggars at each intersection. Most of them were men—some sitting on cardboard boxes, some with signs asking for money. One after the other, I passed them without stopping to give them anything. In New York, where I grew up, there was a mantra about the homeless that went something like this: "Don't give to beggars on the streets. They'll only buy alcohol or drugs with the money."

As I came to the end of a long line of intersections, I stopped at a red light and noticed a young woman a few feet in front of me begging at the corner. She couldn't have been more than eighteen years old, with her long, straggly, dirty-blond hair; a petite, chiseled face; and piercing, light-blue eyes. I could see the outline of her ribs through mismatched, ragged clothes that hung from her emaciated body. Her bony arms were wrapped around a cardboard sign that said, "Please help. I need food and money."

The driver in front of me handed her a can of soda, and I watched while she strained to smile, as if her face muscles could barely command the skin to move. I quickly started rummaging through my purse, hoping the light wouldn't change and cause the drivers behind me to start honking their horns. I whipped out a $5 bill and gently handed it to her, smiled, and wished her a good day. She said thanks and continued walking to approach the car behind me. I immediately wanted to give her more, but traffic had moved on, and I was already on my way. Driving back through that same intersection later that day, I looked for her. She was gone. She was one of thousands of women who live on the streets, some with their children. That day was certainly a reminder to me that life was about a lot more than just me and my own little problems.

When we think about humility, we think about the charity and unselfishness of someone like Mother Teresa—a woman who devoted her life to the poorest of the poor, opened missionary houses all over the world, and never once boasted about winning the Nobel Peace Prize! But humility has two sides. To me, the homeless woman on the street corner was overflowing with humility. She sought the light in others, without realizing that it was actually her own light that attracted them to her. She was a humble goddess.

Five Ways to Eat Humble Pie:

* Know that as soon as you think you're humble, you're not.

* Imagine yourself living the life of someone less fortunate than you.

* Let others shine, and be happy for their success.

* Give others credit when they deserve it.

* Spend more time listening to what others have to say than you spend talking about yourself.

Think it. Say it. Feel it.

I am modest about myself and respect the success and challenges of others.

My personal affirmations to eat humble pie:

. . . .

. . . .

. . . .

. . . .

. . . .

14

Accessorize Your Life

ALL WOMEN KNOW that accessories make the outfit. A boring gray skirt and white button-down shirt can be transformed into a head-turning ensemble when you add a colorful scarf, dangling earrings, red pumps, and a matching leather handbag. Accessories can also provide tremendous enjoyment in life. No, I don't mean jewelry and belts—although a new pair of shoes is like a happy drug for me—but other things that can weave color, emotion, and texture into everyday life.

Your living and working environments, for example, should be a delectable feast for your senses, filled with things you enjoy—a particular piece of art, photos of family and friends, the scent of a fresh rose or spicy vanilla candle, the sound of your favorite jazz CD or water trickling down a small fountain. A few years ago, I created a CD with twenty of my favorite songs, and listening to it always puts me in a good mood—actually, better than good, when

you consider that I start dancing around the house like a wild woman and singing (some might call it yelling) at the top of my lungs.

Friends and family are also accessories, adding layers of social interaction and emotional support to your life. Children are certainly playful additions to anyone's life, and if you mentor a child, you've chosen to be an accessory to her life. And then there are the nonhuman species as well. Pets, with their unconditional love, can make you feel like the most important person on earth. Dogs and other animals are brought into hospitals to lift people's spirits and help the healing process. There are millions of plant species that are just waiting to be part of your life. Go outside and rub your bare feet on a patch of cool grass. Smell a flower. Take a hike. Plant a garden.

One of the biggest accessories to my life is food, not because I need it to survive but because it's so much a part of who I am. Preparing a simple tomato salad is thoroughly enjoying to me: the aroma of basil permeating the room as I tear off the leaves; the wet, firm texture of tomato on my fingers; the colorful spiral of red, white, and green created by alternating slices of tomato, basil, and fresh mozzarella on a platter. After topping it off with salt, pepper, and extra-virgin olive oil, I sit down with friends and family, savoring every bite while I listen and talk to my guests. That one simple salad stimulates all of my senses.

Even ancient goddesses are not without their accessories. Quan Yin, the Chinese goddess of compassion and mercy, is often depicted with items around her symbolizing her role in the world. For example, a vase stands for the pouring out of her compassion to all beings, a lotus blossom represents the purity in our hearts that is always present, and a willow branch reminds us of our ability to bend and adapt without breaking.

Accessories add fun and interest to your life. Could you imagine Elizabeth Taylor without diamonds or any of the *Sex and the City* women without their Cosmopolitan cocktails? Whatever or whoever does it for you—red pumps, a hot fudge sundae, new curtains, your cat, or a favorite song—adding accessories to your life is a guaranteed ticket to many happy moments. The spirit of the goddess inside of you needs to be fed and stimulated so that you can stay excited about life.

Five Ways to Accessorize Your Life:

* Surround yourself with things you love to look at.

* Intermingle frequently with adults, children, animals, and nature.

* Fill your home with the smell of fresh-baked cookies or a meal made from scratch.

* Listen to your favorite music while doing mundane chores.

* Carve out time for a special hobby.

Think it. Say it. Feel it.

I surround my life with people, animals, and things I love.

My personal affirmations to accessorize my life:

....

....

....

....

....

15

Be Nice

HUMAN BEINGS ARE most evolved species on the planet . . . or are we? No other species inflicts such harm on their own kind as we humans do. Sure, there are animals that eat their young or have territorial fights, but for the most part, they play nice. In the animal kingdom, there's no stealing, assault with deadly weapons, and little bullying. I don't know too many animals in therapy and can't think of any other living community where jails are necessary.

I believe people should be kind to one another. Even as a child, I felt the sting of every arrow shot at the kid getting bullied at the back of the school bus. I have recurrent nightmares if I watch a movie with excessive violence. And I don't see the point in reality shows that either humiliate or eliminate people as if they're six-year-olds on a playground.

My rule for dealing with difficult and rude people: Kill 'em with kindness! Yes, of course there are times when I want to retaliate, but I learned that rudeness only begets more rudeness. By being *extra* polite, we make it difficult for most people to continue being nasty. Steven Greenbaum of Passaic, New Jersey, chose not to retaliate after his wife and unborn child were killed by a suicide bomber in Jerusalem. He started an organization called Partners in Kindness with the mission to encourage kindness around the world through the sharing of inspiring stories of good deeds via email. As a result of his efforts, the New York City Transit Department started a kindness public awareness program among employees.

Everyone has the capability to be nice, even the rich and famous; money and fame, by the way, give them no excuse to be inconsiderate to others. Actress Sandra Bullock is one of those famous people about whom you never hear an unkind word. She is known to be friendly to the entire crews on her movie sets and quite the practical joker, too. She treats others with respect and consideration, no matter what their jobs. I suppose art imitated life when her character was given the "Miss Congeniality" award in the movie by the same name.

So, before you skip the "Please" and "Thank you," the friendly smiles, the kind favors, and the whole damn practice of kindness, look down within yourself and find that well of natural compassion all goddesses have. It may be a little dry, but you can easily replenish it by remembering why you're here—not because you're fully evolved but because you're only halfway there. Until we learn to be better and kinder human beings, we'll always be one evolution step below those seemingly primitive animals.

Five Ways to Be Nice:

* Work to understand the perspective of people you consider adversaries.

* Every day, give someone a compliment or do a small favor for them.

* Don't respond to rudeness with more rudeness—be kinder or be quiet.

* Ask yourself how YOU would feel if treated a certain way—if you don't like it, don't treat others that way!

* Look people in the eyes and smile when speaking to them.

Think it. Say it. Feel it.

I am compassionate and pleasant to every person I encounter.

My personal affirmations to be nice:

....

....

....

....

....

16

Get Physical

WHENEVER I WATCH an athlete perform, I'm reminded of the incredible potential of the human body. Olympic medalist Jackie Joyner-Kersee is said to be the best all-around female athlete in the world. Running the hurdles in the Games, she was a symbol of strength *and* grace, commanding her well-defined muscles to propel her body with the explosive power of a Ferrari on a race track. Of course, not every woman's body is destined to be a Ferrari, but the least we can do is aim for a well-oiled, dependable, and long-lasting Honda.

Before workout videos became popular, I can remember exercising on the living room rug with my mother when I was just a child. Perhaps that kick-started my lifelong passion and desire for regular exercise. I used to run up and down steps to keep fit in my teens (well before stair machines); I started weight lifting in high school, I taught aerobics in college, and I'm sure I was one of the first women to buy in-line skates in the early eighties.

It's important to pick an exercise you love to do. I recently purchased a thirteen-foot trampoline for exercise and play. (I've wanted one my entire life, and since I was over forty, I figured I was finally old enough to have one!) As soon as I start jumping, I start laughing and immediately forget that I'm actually doing a workout. And then there is dancing. I went from being a child taking tap and jazz classes to a pre-teen dancing to seventies' rock and roll to a disco queen in the eighties. I eventually settled on tribal dancing as my thing. Although I still do a regular routine of aerobic activity and weight training, it's music and the primal beat of the drum that feeds my soul, making my body move in the most unusual and yet instinctively natural ways and transporting me to a time of ritualistic ceremony and spiritual connection to Mother Earth. I even bought my own drum and often use it in meditation to quiet my mind, connecting the beat of my heart with the heart of the earth.

Exercise of all kinds should be an integral part of your everyday life, like brushing your teeth. Sure, there are times when you won't be motivated to work out or you're sick or overscheduled, and you'll stop for a few days, but hopefully you'll start missing that euphoric feeling enough to want to start it up again. If you think of exercise as just a little extra movement you incorporate into your everyday life, it becomes easy to fit in—a power walk with your dog, a yoga class, or a game of tag with the kids. Just like the car that runs better and lasts longer with proper maintenance, a goddess's body needs care. So find your own dance and start dancing!

Five Ways to Get Physical:

* If you're not disciplined to exercise on your own, do it with a girlfriend.

* Choose the kind of exercise you enjoy and make a habit of it.

* Don't sit more than twenty minutes without getting up and moving.

* Try out a new active sport or class (yoga, tennis, or even tap dancing).

* Pay attention to your daily activities and do more of those that move your body.

Think it. Say it. Feel it.

I keep my body healthy with daily movement and regular exercise.

My personal affirmations to get physical:

....

....

....

....

....

17

Ask for Help

THERE'S AN OPENING song from the TV sitcom *Scrubs* that says, "I can't do it all on my own. No, I'm no Superman." Most women spend their entire lives trying to prove that statement wrong (with the exception of a gender change from Superman to Super-woman) when, in fact, if we only accepted it as the truth, life would be so much easier. If we take a look back at the way families were raised just a few generations ago, people lived and worked close to other family members whom they relied upon for care and support. In the indigenous tribes still existing today around the world, the entire tribe acts as the family support system. There's a saying, "It takes a village to raise a child," but how many mothers today ask the villagers for help?

Many women equate *having* it all with *handling* it all—by themselves, from successful careers to perfect homes. There's no need for anyone to open doors for them even if their arms are wrapped around two stuffed bags of groceries with a purse trailing off their

shoulders—they can just kick that door open with their feet and shove their body and bags through it! The unfortunate part of all this is that people actually want to help.

I have a friend whom I've known since high school. She and her family live only two miles away from me, and while I consider her as close as a sister to me, I don't see her often since she's raising four children (ages three to twelve). We often rely on email to keep in touch. One day, she responded to one of my "Hi, how are you doing?" emails and said she was just getting back to normal after the surgery. Surgery . . . what surgery, I thought. How did I not know about this? I could have helped. I could have been there for her. We later chatted, and she said she just didn't think to ask me.

During a time when I was launching a new business—I had been at it for four years and had exhausted all avenues for sufficiently paying work without any indication that my luck would change— I was at the crossroads between going back to my old line of work or continuing on my own. Other than my husband and a few close friends, no one knew how much I was struggling financially and emotionally.

In a session with a spiritual consultant, I learned that hiding my vulnerability was like erecting a solid brick wall around myself that was actually intimidating to people. No one would dare to enter, let alone offer to help. Upon the consultant's suggestion, I did something that was very uncomfortable and foreign to me. I started explaining my situation to people and asking for help in specific areas. Revealing my inner struggles, failures, and imperfections was

a painstaking process, as I'd always taken pride in my emotional strength and ability to create success around me. Afterward, a couple of my friends told me that they admired my honesty, courage, and willingness to bare it all. Within a month, two part-time opportunities came my way, which paved the way for more work later on.

Girls grow up yearning for independence, wanting to make it on our own, but sometimes we wake up one day as the lone wolf in the forest looking for our own food, nursing our own wounds, and watching our own back for predators. All goddesses need help sometime in their lives. Know that the help you seek is out there, but it won't come until you ask. You'll be surprised to find out how many willing and able people really do want to help you.

Five Ways to Ask for Help:

* Open up and confide in someone.

* Pray or meditate, asking God, the Goddess, angels, or other spirit guides to help you.

* Seek professional help if you think you need it (through therapy, counseling, or with your medical doctor).

* Offer to help others in need, knowing the universe will return help to you when you need it.

* Feel grateful, not guilty, when someone helps you.

Think it. Say it. Feel it.

I always seek and find help when I need it.

My personal affirmations to ask for help:

....

....

....

....

....

18

Have an Adventure

ADVENTURE IS HAVING the courage to take risks without the anxiety of being judged negatively or failing. If Columbus cared about his reputation, he would've played it safe and stuck to the flat-world theory. And, if nobody took any chances, who knows when someone would have discovered the medical benefits of penicillin from bread mold? How dull life would be without adventure!

In 1998, five breast cancer survivors and seven Princeton University women (ages twenty-two through sixty-one) climbed Alaska's Mount McKinley to raise money for breast cancer research. Although some of them had mountaineering experience, most didn't—they were teachers, therapists, farmers, and tennis instructors.

While most of us may not ever climb a 20,000-foot mountain (I can safely say I won't), there are still smaller adventures we can have to spice up our lives. When I was thirty-eight years old, I walked into a tattoo shop with a drawing of a sun, moon, and star to be etched into my ankle. It was like a rite of passage for me, ushering in the

next stage of my life. I had left a fifteen-year career behind with no idea where I was going or how to get there, yet the anticipation of new possibilities was exciting. Some friends and colleagues thought I was insane to quit a successful career, but I listened to a voice inside me that beckoned like a blinking lighthouse to a ship in a misty fog. It said, "Do it, do it, DO IT."

It was that same voice that encouraged me to move 3,000 miles away from home when I was twenty-three and to elope at twenty-six. These decisions were not the most popular with my Italian American parents—okay, they were devastated by my actions! They believed a woman's place was in the kitchen . . . serving her father until she got married to serve her husband. They believed in making all the safe choices in life, just as they had—a philosophy that was guaranteed to lead to a life of unhappiness, just like theirs.

Many parents discourage adventure to protect their children from disappointment. As a girl, I felt like a dog behind an invisible fence. Each time I was tempted to go beyond the line, I felt a shock to the back of my neck, usually in the form of my father's voice saying, "What are you—an idiot? You'll kill yourself doing that!" Thankfully, there were many times in my life when my spirit of adventure outweighed the memory of my father's advice and drove me forward, even if it was only to show him that not everyone who skis breaks a leg! And if I did break a leg, at least I was doing something I enjoyed. Award-winning novelist Erica Jong said, "And the trouble is, if you don't risk anything, you risk even more."

And, if you're ever thinking about getting a tattoo, make it easy

like I did and get a prescription for analgesic (numbing) cream. A goddess shouldn't need to include pain in her adventure!

Five Ways to Have an Adventure:

* Take the path in life you want, not the one others expect you to take.

* Turn fear into excitement by visualizing the best outcome of a risky decision.

* Commit to trying something new—twice a year.

* Don't listen to naysayers; they're secretly jealous of adventurers.

* Change a familiar routine—your morning ritual, the drive to work, Saturday gardening.

> ### Think it. Say it. Feel it.
> *I am ready and willing to have exciting experiences in my life.*

My personal affirmations to have an adventure:

....

....

....

....

19

Enjoy the Journey

ONCE IN MAUI, two girlfriends and I set out to find a quiet beach for the day. Not a touristy beach crowded with families, honeymooners, and the smell of coconut suntan lotion, but a small private patch of sand where we could talk and connect with Mother Nature. We hopped into our rental car at 11 A.M. Without an itinerary, we wanted to rely on our natural instincts and, of course, on Maui's resident volcano goddess, Pele, to show us the way.

After passing all the familiar beaches, we continued along the main road, stopping at various spots. Some of these were quite picturesque, with crashing waves hitting jagged black lava rock; however, they were not exactly what we had in mind. As our journey progressed, the wide, flat, double-lane highway turned into a single-lane, broken tarred road with hairpin turns leading up a mountain. Moving at five miles per hour, we had to honk the horn around each turn to alert possible drivers coming in the opposite

direction. Yes, it was a bit treacherous but highly worth the breath-taking ocean and cliff views.

After a couple of hours, our stomachs were grumbling from the winding road *and* our mounting hunger. One friend remembered that this was the road that led to a small town where an old woman sold homemade banana bread from a roadside hut. Nothing (except maybe chocolate) could have been a better incentive for three goddesses to continue onward than the prospect of finding that banana bread lady!

An hour and a few dozen switchback turns later, we found her, a Hawaiian native with island hair and an ear-to-ear smile—she looked as if she had been waiting for us all along! We devoured the banana bread and conceded that it *was* the best banana bread we had ever tasted—warm, moist, spicy, and sweet. When we asked our hostess if we should turn back, she recommended that we continue on the same road since we were more than halfway around the mountain and the road would eventually circle back to the beach.

With happy, full tummies, we headed out. Finally, after several towns, the road took one last curve, leading us back to blue water. At 4 P.M., we noticed a small beach covered with trees that grew out of the sand and bent toward the ocean at unusual angles. We settled into that secluded beach, swam in the crystal-clear ocean, gave each other tarot card readings, and soaked up the sun until 5:30 P.M., when we had to leave.

Imagine our surprise when we arrived at the hotel ten minutes later! We had traveled most of the day looking for the perfect beach, only to find it ten minutes from where we started. Yes, sometimes what you're looking for is right under your own nose, but that beach would have never looked and felt as good had we found it in ten minutes. We would have missed the journey—beautiful scenery, intimate conversations, and yes . . . the best banana bread in the world! Maybe Pele really *was* leading us.

Regardless of your destination, it's the journey that gives it meaning.

Five Ways to Enjoy the Journey:

* On family car trips, take time to stop along the way to absorb the scenery or the people.

* When you set a goal in life, accept and enjoy any and all roads that lead to it.

* When you reach a goal in life, reflect upon the lessons learned in your journey and appreciate what you've accomplished.

* Keep a daily journal and read past entries. They will answer your questions about why things happened when they did.

* When a difficult situation takes you off track, stay in the present, knowing that this, too, shall pass.

Think it. Say it. Feel it.

I acknowledge the significance of every step I take in life.

My personal affirmations to enjoy the journey:

....

....

....

....

....

20

Forgive and Forget

HAVE YOU EVER made a mistake? Of course you have. We all have! If you were the only one affected by the mistake, you might just consider yourself foolish. If your mistake caused harm or inconvenience to another person, you might choose to apologize. If someone caused you harm, you might decide to forgive them. In either situation, you need to make one last choice—to forgive yourself or not.

Women often talk about forgiveness as it relates to forgiving others, but forgiveness starts with ourselves first. Of all the prejudices and stubborn opinions we harbor, we save the most judgmental and condemning for ourselves. "I should've, could've, would've . . . I can't get anything right . . . I'm no good." Women are known to say, "I'm sorry" habitually, as if they were responsible for every problem in the world. Even for the smallest infractions that shouldn't warrant a second thought—like eating that piece of chocolate cake that

wasn't on the diet—we refuse to forgive ourselves, causing considerable damage to our self-worth.

If we're not accustomed to forgiving ourselves, it's difficult to forgive others. When my younger sister committed suicide in her early twenties, I imploded with guilt. I hated myself for not being able to prevent her death, and I hated my sister for causing my family so much pain. Then I hated myself even more for hating her! The months following her death were filled with depression, anxiety, and a depth of sadness so dark that I felt as if I were living in a thick black cloud of smoke, smoldering in its putrid fumes. I finally decided to see a family counselor. After a couple of months, I was able to rise above the cloud of darkness, but only after I forgave my sister *and* myself for our mistakes. I learned that I couldn't continue to blame myself for another person's actions and that forgiveness instantly lightens a heavy heart.

In an ABC News interview with Barbara Walters, Hillary Clinton (who, most women would agree, had plenty of cause to be angry for eternity after the very public Monica Lewinsky scandal involving her husband) said, "I reached the point where I decided that I was either going to have to forgive . . . and let go of the anger and the disappointment that I had felt, or we weren't going to have a marriage. . . . And both of us worked very, very hard to reach that point. . . . The counseling . . . led me to believe that this was a marriage and a love that I wanted to try to preserve if it could be. And I was willing to try."

By holding on to hate and blame for the people who harm us, we may feel like the keepers of justice, but all we're really doing is stoking the coals of a dangerous fire burning within us. A fire that quickly destroys any love or humanity we may have left. While justice and the law should prevail when someone commits a criminal act, the human heart still needs to heal when someone or something injures it. Fire won't heal it—love and forgiveness will.

Each experience you have in life is a lesson, especially those that are most damaging to you. You can't predict or know what someone else's lessons in life are, and, therefore, you can't judge other people for what they might do—even if they hurt you. Once you forgive yourself and others, you can let go of the pain *and* the past.

Five Ways to Forgive and Forget:

* Find the lesson in your mistakes and then move on.

* Apologize when you've hurt another person.

* Know that all people are capable of love, even when their actions say otherwise.

* Know that forgiving a person brings peace of mind for oneself.

* If a person causes you emotional pain, tell her or him.

Think it. Say it. Feel it.

My heart overflows with forgiveness for myself and others.

My personal affirmations to forgive and forget:

....

....

....

....

....

21

Lighten Up!

From a very young age, girls are taught to be responsible, which often translates into being serious like adults. Boys (or men) can be boys; however, girls are expected to be women. We become experts in drama but never really learn the ins and outs of comedy. Have you ever been around someone who can laugh at her own shortcomings, find humor in any situation, and make you laugh as well? Ellen Degeneres comes to my mind. She once did a monologue on her talk show about a fortune cookie she received one night at dinner; the fortune said, "It makes you happy to make people happy." She went on to say that she gets hundreds of letters from people telling her that they love watching her show because it makes them happy. Who wouldn't get happy after listening to Ellen joke about herself or the happenings of everyday life? Women like Ellen have a unique talent and provide a special gift to humanity; they help lighten the load in life by showing us a more balanced, less serious perspective.

Sometimes you can feel a great emotional release by laughing in the most stressful situations. Have you ever had the urge to laugh uncontrollably at the most inappropriate times, such as when you're at a funeral or when someone falls? I've laughed in both those scenarios. Scientific studies show that laughter can boost the immune system and alleviate stress by releasing endorphins in the brain. After prescribing laughing to his patients, the Indian doctor Madan Kataria founded the first laughter club in 1995. A 2003 article in *Health* magazine reported that there are now over sixty laughter clubs in the United States.

In her book *I'd Rather Laugh*, Linda Richman (the real person behind the *Saturday Night Live* character in "Coffee Talk with Linda Richman," a skit created by Richman's son-in-law, Mike Myers) talks about losing her father at eight years old; being raised by her mentally ill mother, who was eventually institutionalized; losing her twenty-nine-year-old son in a car accident; and having to spend eleven years inside her apartment because she suffered from agoraphobia. She says, "No matter what horrible thing has happened, life still offers you humor if you want it. Regardless of how low you feel today, someday you'll find something that will make you laugh your head off." Through her writing and workshops, she helps others find the inherent humor in everyday life.

Something that always lightens me up is watching reruns of the TV show *Bewitched*, where anything is possible with just a twitch of the nose or a wave of the hand from Samantha Stephens, the happy good witch with extraordinary powers and charm who lights up a room with her smile and wit. Her all-too-serious and worrisome husband, Darrin, doesn't ever figure out how much fun life could be if he just allowed Samantha to fully unleash the power of the goddess within her. The show is a good reminder to bring out the Samantha inside of us as often as possible.

Next time you start magnifying and internalizing all of your problems, as we all do from time to time, listen to the goddess inside. I'm sure she's telling you, "Twitch your nose and lighten up, already!"

Five Ways to Lighten Up:

* In difficult times, find isolated moments that are funny, regardless of the big picture.

* Give yourself permission to laugh and have fun in any circumstance.

* Watch funny movies and TV shows and appreciate the masters at work.

* Don't take yourself, your ego, or job too seriously—they can all be gone tomorrow.

* Try to get a baby to laugh—watch and listen to how funny you can be!

Think it. Say it. Feel it.

I find laughter within me no matter what is happening outside of me.

My personal affirmations to lighten up:

....

....

....

....

....

22

Be Rich

How rich is rich enough for you—millionaire, billionaire, trillionaire? Someone from the ghettos of New York City might think that having a swimming pool makes you rich. A person living in an impoverished third world country might consider anyone with running water to be rich. It's all relative.

We learn early on that money and material possessions define how rich we are. We also learn that we never have enough of either of these. Walk into the home of any middle-class family with children these days and take a look at the toy collection. Chances are, you won't find a crate full of toys, but a roomful! How many birthday parties have you been to where you've watched a child frantically tear the wrapping off a gift (as if a bomb would explode if it weren't opened in ten seconds), only to fling the present off to the side in order to get to the next one? Hence the pattern begins, a habit of wanting more while never feeling like you have enough.

Of course, we should know deep down inside that money isn't the only measurement of richness in life, but, alas, we live in a society where advertisements, news media, and retail stores paint a different picture—one with large green dollar signs against a backdrop of colorful merchandise and subliminal promises of happiness and success. There's nothing wrong with wanting and having it all. The problem exists when we make earning money and acquiring possessions our top and only priorities in life. That's when it turns ugly; people get greedy and use unscrupulous methods to get want they want. Look at what happened during the booming economy of the mid- to late nineties: wealthy business people, stockbrokers, and well-known media personalities were convicted of trying to amass even *more* money with their white-collar crimes.

Here's a news flash: You can be as rich a woman as you want in life; there is plenty of abundance in the universe for everyone. You may need to adjust your definition of what "rich" is to you and certainly expand that definition to include other things besides money and possessions—love, respect, friendship, admiration, happiness . . . to name a few. When you do that, you'll realize how abundant your life really is, and your perception of your resources will immediately change—instead of seeing what you lack or need, you'll see how well off you are. Universal law goes like this: Like attracts like. You will attract more riches into your life, including money, if you already see yourself as rich. Maybe in the end you'll decide that you have enough money. Maybe you'll decide you deserve more. Either

way, you're more likely to have and receive money if you approach life with an attitude of abundance rather than one of poverty.

Call upon Lakshmi, the Hindu goddess of abundance, beauty, and happiness, to help you build both your material *and* spiritual wealth, as both are equally important. Lakshmi is said to have been born, fully grown, out of the ocean on a lotus petal and adorned with precious jewels, gold, and gifts. There is a chant you can use to invoke the presence of Lakshmi: "Om Nameh, Lakshmi Namah." She is always available to bring good fortune to others . . . that includes you, goddess!

Five Ways to Be Rich:

* Count your blessings in all areas of your life every day.

* Celebrate successes with friends and family.

* Visualize having what you desire, rather than focusing on not having it.

* Don't compare your life or money with that of another— we each have a unique path.

* Always place a higher value on love than money.

> ### Think it. Say it. Feel it.
> *My life is overflowing with abundance, prosperity, and success.*

My personal affirmations to be rich:

....

....

....

....

....

23

Rise above Fear

FEAR IS EVERYWHERE you go, in every event, in every person. Turn on the nightly news and you'll get an ample dose of daily fear—murderers on the loose, outbreaks of infectious diseases, terrorist warnings, dangerous weather conditions, tainted food supplies. And that's just the first fifteen minutes! You might as well assume the fetal position and stay in bed the rest of your life. That is, if you don't have a carbon monoxide leak in your home or an allergic reaction to dust mites. You can find fear in anything . . . if that's what you're looking for.

The media loves fear because fear sells more papers, attracts more viewers, and gives the media outlets a captive audience. When a friend of mine shut off the dismal TV news at her dying grandmother's house one day, her grandmother quickly reprimanded her and yelled, "Turn the news back on. I have to know if there's anything I need to worry about!" She died about a month later.

Control is at the root of effort to instill fear in others; a fear-mongering media often renders its victims emotionally paralyzed. Many battered women continue to suffer at the hands of their controlling spouses or partners for fear of the consequences of an unsuccessful exit—or perhaps just for fear of the unknown, a feeling we've all experienced around issues such as safety, money, relationships, health, or salvation. (The fear of God has long been used as a tactic for religious groups to corral their parishioners into supporting the groups' beliefs *and* contributing to their wealth.)

After her home was bombed, the lives of her children threatened, and her husband murdered, Coretta Scott King (the wife of Martin Luther King, Jr.) could have easily chosen to live a more quiet, normal life, but just four days after her husband's death, she led a march of 50,000 people and then continued to carry on his work as a human rights advocate, helping millions of others to choose nonviolent means for social change.

Much of what happens in the world and in your life is out of your immediate control, but you do have control over how you choose to deal with these events. In a TV interview, actress Fran Drescher talked about her scary experience with uterine cancer. She said, "I had my moments when I got very frightened that I would not recover. At night, when you do not have the distractions of the day, sometimes you connect dots that aren't even there. But my friend Elaine very wisely advised me not to mix imagination with fear. It's a deadly cocktail." Fran survived her cancer and later wrote a book about her experience, *Cancer Schmancer*, to help other women face their fears.

Imagine how much energy it takes to focus on the worst possible scenario of every day. Now imagine channeling that energy in a positive direction, making your life more fun, happy, and fulfilling. While you can't change what's presented to you by your friends, family, community, and the world—either individually or through mass communication—you can change how you react to it—or don't. If something happens that doesn't please you, choose to be a goddess and rise above it, without stopping to visit.

Five Ways to Rise Above Fear:

* Learn not to worry about things you can't control or things that *might* happen.

* Detach yourself from the negative emotional hype of media news, or don't watch it.

* If you feel threatened in any relationship, leave or seek help.

* Visualize yourself bathed in protective white light wherever you are.

* Remember there are two sides to every story—find the positive one.

Think it. Say it. Feel it.

I am protected wherever I go in life, physically, emotionally, and financially.

My personal affirmations to rise above fear:

....

....

....

....

....

24

Pick Something... Anything

IN THE COURSE of an average day, we make hundreds of decisions. In a week, thousands. In a lifetime, hundreds of thousands—ranging from what to wear on a particular day to whom to marry for the rest of our lives. Granted, the daily trivial choices become an invisible backdrop to the more important decisions in life, such as having a child or choosing a career. Or to the more emotionally packed choices, like getting a divorce or removing life support for a loved one. While the big decisions in life are the ones that we remember most, even the seemingly simple ones can become complicated and time-consuming for many women, especially when we automatically attach an expectation of "right" or "wrong," which forces us to evaluate constantly whether or not we made the *correct* choice. Any inkling of doubt can cause tremendous unhappiness.

I have a girlfriend who agonizes over every decision. She once won one of those raffles at a charity event where you go up to a table filled with free stuff and pick whatever you want. While she was deciding, three other raffle winners were called, and they naturally picked some of the better gifts. Finally, my friend made a choice (as pickings were getting slim), only to go back to her seat and rethink her decision, including why she should have chosen one of the other gifts!

In discussing decisions versus choices, another friend of mine said, "Life is so complicated and stressful because we confuse making choices with making decisions. Decisions are made by passing judgment between two or more variables and assigning a right or a wrong in order to make up one's mind. Choices are a selection—there is no weight or right/wrong assigned to the choice." When you are deciding between wearing the gray suit or the red dress, you have no way of predicting how wearing one instead of the other will play out that day. Therefore, you are only able to make a selection at that moment.

Yes, there are larger choices in a women's life that do take some time and thought to make, but once you do make them, it's important to release your attachment to any outcome; it's particularly vital to know that you can't go back in time. You may decide to change your choice in the future if conditions allow—after all, a goddess has the right to change her mind—but then again, that's just another choice you make at that moment in time. If you live your life in a tactical, decision-making battleground, constantly trying to make the perfect decision that will result in *your* version of success every time, you'll be guaranteed a lot of bloodshed . . . most of it your own. However, if you perceive life as a series of personal choices, you will realize that every choice you make has a purpose in your life, even those choices that steer you in unpleasant directions. Every failure and every success in life happen at exactly the right time because every choice a goddess makes is perfect.

Five Ways to Pick Something . . . Anything:

* Once you make a choice, accept it and move on—don't keep wondering "what if."

* Ask yourself, "What's the worst that could happen from this choice?" It's usually nothing that can't be fixed or forgotten about.

* Remember that in some cases you can choose *not* to make any choice.

* Don't fall into the "paralysis by analysis" syndrome— you'll never be able to make any choices if you think too much.

* Don't assign a right or wrong to every choice—consider them all viable options.

Think it. Say it. Feel it.

I am confident in my choices and easily make decisions.

My personal affirmations to pick something . . . anything:

....

....

....

....

....

25

Play!

WHEN WAS THE last time you played? I'm not talking about watching TV game shows or playing in some game at work where stress and humiliation are skillfully masked under the guise of motivational fun. I'm talking about an enjoyable activity with no agenda, no timeframe, and no anxiety about how messy you get or how foolish you look. Something you choose to do, not something you have to do. Playing to play, not to win.

Often on the journey from childhood to adulthood, we forget how and why to play. One day we wake up . . . grown up! It's as if there's some mysterious inner tour guide in our head saying, "It's now time to leave Barbie and her pink camper behind and enter the real world of serious thinkers and doers." Hence, a long stretch of all work and no play begins. (Remember the psycho Jack Nicholson became in *The Shining* when *that* happened!)

But we don't have to give up on our inner child so easily. One day, while I was walking by a park near my home with Joe and our

dogs, we repeated a dialogue we had had a number of times while passing this park.

I said, "I used to love to go on the swings when I was a kid."

He said, "So why don't you?"

I said, "Me? Here? I would look silly."

But on this day, all the swings were empty, and when he nudged me again, I decided to go for it. I sat my butt down on the flexible seat (*hmmm, a lot cushier than my childhood swing set, which consisted of hard metal seats with steel posts loosely anchored to the ground by a chunk of cement that dangerously lifted off the grass when you went high*). I started the motions of bending and straightening my legs, gradually adding height and speed. (It's like riding a bike—you never forget.) Within seconds, I felt that familiar rush of wind in my hair and a tickling in my belly. As I got higher, I started laughing out loud and yelled down to Joe, like a five-year-old, "Look, I can touch the sky!" When I was ready to come down, I gently scraped my feet on the soft brown bark below me, slowing down just enough for a flying dismount. *I could still do it! I was young again.* That was my first of many visits to my neighborhood swing set—just for the fun of it!

Play is so easy to do (after all, kids can do it sixteen hours a day), and it doesn't have to cost much. Next time you're in a toy department, spend a couple bucks, and buy a brightly colored, or perhaps striped, hula hoop. It's guaranteed to provide loads of laughter, either when you're by yourself (watching in a mirror, of course) or when your friends come to visit. It will take you awhile to get the hang of it again, so here's a hint: angle it lower in the front and make the first swing slower than you think you need. Then let the gyrating begin!

A goddess is never too old to play. Remember Cyndi Lauper's 1983 hit song, "Girls Just Want to Have Fun"? In 2003, at fifty years old, Cyndi was still performing that song on tour. I happened to catch her on a VH1 *Divas Live* special in 2004; she was a delight to watch—still singing, dancing, and smiling . . . still having fun.

Five Ways to Play:

* Take a break to play with your kids—play a board game, bicycle, run around the backyard, or jump in rain puddles.

* Make ordinary household chores playful (sing silly made-up songs while you're doing them, or have a pillow fight with your bed-making partner).

* Make a list of your favorite childhood games or activities and commit to doing one of them weekly.

* When you're especially stressed at work, distract yourself for a few minutes with something mindless (doodle, walk outside, pick a flower).

* Once in awhile, honor your inner child by playing first and working later.

Think it. Say it. Feel it.

I honor my inner child with joyful playtime.

My personal affirmations to play:

....

....

....

....

....

26

Make Connections

CAN YOU IMAGINE those peer-pressured, awkward years in high school without someone to talk to—a best girlfriend, a sister, or a radical aunt? Ironically, that's the time when you're most centered on yourself, and yet that's precisely when you need to connect with others. In the book *Girlfriends*, authors Carmen Renee Berry and Tamara Traeder state, "They (girlfriends) are not only essential for coping with our day-to-day frustrations or sharing private jokes, they help us limp through a crisis and, in the long run, help us grow as women and human beings."

While there is an inherent emphasis in our society on individuality, a woman's path in life is not meant to be traveled by a lone goddess. The connections you make with others, whether they are friends, family, or strangers, are what give your life meaning. With the exception of some religious orders, in which monks vow to live in solitude, we generally need other people (or at least a pet) to add texture to our lives. Studies show that social connections have a

positive effect on our well-being. Research noted in the *Girlfriends* book proves that a woman's development is very much tied to the personal connections she makes in life, whereas a man's development relies more upon his independence and self-reliance.

Some say the Internet is the ultimate connection for everyone in the world. The Internet cannot, however, replace companionship, because it disconnects you from emotion and spirit—two important feminine traits. Email can never replace the spectrum of emotions created by the physical interaction with another human being. The Internet will not teach your children how to listen to the sound of a voice with their hearts or how to hug a friend who is hurting.

Face-to-face connection with others is nourishment for your soul as much as food and water are for your body. A couple of years ago, I started attending a woman's meditation group thanks to a "connection" from my good friend Jenai, who happened to meet Simone, the woman who leads the group, at a book signing and then told me about her. (Jenai and I got connected while volunteering for a nonprofit teen girls' event and then became close friends.) The women in the meditation group represented a wide range of ages (from twenties to sixties) and spiritual beliefs (from Buddhist to Christian). Most of them didn't know each other before joining the group. When we meet, we spend timing chatting about what's going on in our lives, eating, choosing tarot cards, and, of course, meditating. I don't usually see any of these women outside of our group, and yet I feel closer to them than some friends I've had all my life. We are supportive of one another, nonjudgmental, and very much connected on a spiritual level as women and as goddesses. I try never to miss my meditation group, because I always leave with a full and grateful heart. Like chocolate, I crave that interaction, and sometimes I get to have both. In fact, one night, each of us brought one chocolate dessert to share!

The connections you make during your time on earth are like a million lifelines floating in a vast ocean—each with its own unique life preserver, only a thought away from embracing you. When your world is turned upside down and you want to crawl into a shell, the best thing you can do is reach out for one of those lifelines. Helen Keller said, "Walking with a friend in the dark is better than walking alone in the light." All it takes is your desire to connect.

Five Ways to Make Connections:

* Make small talk with a stranger.

* Research your family tree and call a long-lost relative.

* Join a group that meets regularly—a mother's club, meditation class, women's group.

* Phone a girlfriend you don't see often—rather than sending an email.

* Spend quality time with your family.

Think it. Say it. Feel it.

*I pursue and enjoy relationships with family, friends,
and even strangers.*

My personal affirmations to make connections:

....

....

....

....

....

27

Find the Balance

FOR YEARS, THE media has led the charge on the importance of balancing work, life, and family, particularly for women, who are still the main caretakers of the house and family, regardless of whether they work outside the home or not. A few years ago, I was convinced that I had it all under control. Working in the fast-paced, high-stress world of high tech, climbing the corporate ladder of success, I still managed to eat healthy, exercise daily, entertain friends, remember birthdays, and take vacations. Then, when my family started to fall apart due to illness and death, I successfully lived two separate lives with the skill of a juggler watching one ball in the air and one in the hand. In one life, I went in and out of corporate boardrooms doing business presentations, and in the other I was in and out of hospital rooms dealing with doctors.

I certainly felt capable of gracefully handling it all—just like the famous women I read about in the media. Kelly Ripa has a loving marriage with a handsome hubby, three kids, and two daily TV

gigs—one as a talk show host and one as a soap opera actress and then sitcom star. Maria Shriver is a dedicated wife to a famous actor and politician (Arnold Schwarzenegger) and an involved mother to four children, along with her duties as a TV reporter (until she replaced that job with being the first lady to the governor of California), a best-selling author, and one of Oprah's best friends (I'm sure that comes with a lot of time and commitment).

Although most of us are not famous, many people with and without children, like Kelly and Maria, look as though they effortlessly achieved what most women strive for their entire lives—balance. But this isn't reality. After all, in her book *Ten Things I Wish I'd Known—Before I Went Out into the Real World*, Maria Shriver states that Superwoman is dead, and we can't do it all. The only thing that's balanced in our lives is the equal amount of daily stress we experience with work and family life. We continually feed our egos with finished lists, job kudos, or the perfect home and hearth. But the more our egos get fed and the more busy our lives seem, the more our spirits are starved.

For me, the symptoms of a depleted spirit became harder to ignore: my health started to suffer, and my mind started to wander. For those reasons, I walked away at the peak of my career. I did not do consulting part time. I did not take another job. (I did not pass GO and collect $200!) There was no middle ground that would get my equilibrium back. I was too far out, like a fishing line tangled in a bed of muddied seaweed. The only solution was to cut the line and start over. That's when I embarked on a whole new

life-and-work journey that was truly balanced—nurturing my body, mind, and spirit . . . and a lot of other women.

My friend Susan runs her own communications business out of her home, overseeing a handful of employees while also raising five girls, ages three to fourteen. Her job and clients are demanding and time-consuming, so in order to give her family equal time, she utilizes her excellent management skills and applies them to her home life. She specifically carves out dedicated time on her calendar to spend with individual children or for family activities. Whether it's taking a knitting class with one of her girls or planning a family trip with the whole gang, she makes it part of her everyday schedule. If she were to wait until her work is over (which it never is), there would be no time left to spend with the family she loves.

Companies will be bought and sold. Work will come and go. This is the temporary nature of the world in which we live. You must remember that who you are in life is not what you do for a living. The key to balance in life is creating harmony between our spirit, which is eternal, and our physical life, which is finite. When you nurture the goddess within you (your spirit), you will easily and willingly balance, prioritize, and share your life.

Five Ways to Find the Balance:

* Take up a hobby that has nothing to do with your job.

* Feed your spirit regularly—meditate, get a massage, exercise, write, paint, sing.

* Don't be connected to work twenty-four hours a day just because you can be.

* Socialize outside of work, with family, friends, and pets!

* Never miss, postpone, or cancel vacation time.

> **Think it. Say it. Feel it.**
>
> *I easily divide my time and energy between work, play, and sleep.*

My personal affirmations to find the balance:

....

....

....

....

....

28

Make Peace, Not War

LIKE MANY YOUNG girls, I loved watching beauty pageants, especially when they got down to the last few contestants and the big question at the end. It seemed that no matter what the question, "world peace" was the right answer. I truly believed those dazzling women would someday make the world a better place!

I was only three years old when the Vietnam War started in 1964. It wasn't until 1969 that I started to understand what was going on. At eight years old, I willingly did my share for the peace movement. I drew peace symbols all over my homemade schoolbook covers, right alongside my flower power stickers. I didn't know anyone in the war, but I did hear enough to know that people were dying and many were missing in action. I never knew how my parents felt about the war—they never talked about it in front of us— but when my sister and I asked for POW/MIA bracelets, they didn't hesitate to buy them for us. I proudly put my shiny metal bracelet

on every morning and carefully placed it upon my dresser each night. In the evenings, I'd say a prayer for my guy, and during the day, my girlfriends and I would search through the list of found POWs and MIAs in the newspaper. We used to chat about our guys as if they were family.

At that time, I had no comprehension of the political backdrop for the war or of who was winning, nor did I care. The only thing that mattered to me was the safe return of my guy and all the guys over there, wherever "there" might be. Children have a natural ability to cut through the illusions created by adult egos and to see what really matters, in the purest sense. I knew that people were being killed and that homes, villages, and the earth were being destroyed. I knew that was wrong. As human beings, we all come from the same source of pure love, and that's what connects us in spirit. By killing one another, we kill a part of ourselves—the human race.

After the Vietnam War was over, I stopped wearing my bracelet. It had become dented and scratched over the years, the name barely visible anymore. I kept it in a box on top of my dresser until I left home at twenty-three years old, eleven years after the war had ended. I never knew if my guy ever came home—alive or dead.

More recently, in the documentary movie *Fahrenheit 9/11*, I was reminded again that war not only destroys physical people and things, but also desecrates the human spirit. I was reminded of how senseless and wrong it is. And how nobody ever wins. I watched an American mother in agonizing grief over the son she lost, and on the other side of the world, an Iraqi woman was screaming and crying in the name of Allah after her home was bombed. How could any human ever justify this?

When asked, most of us—especially women—would say that we want world peace, but we don't always realize that peace doesn't start out there in the world somewhere, with a particular country or a political leader. It begins inside each and every individual person. A good place to start is to find the goddess within you, making sure that you are at peace inside first—at peace in your body, your spirit, and your life. Then, and only then, can you bring peace to others—from family to friends to strangers to community to country, and finally to the world.

While I don't watch beauty pageants anymore, I do give those goddess contestants credit for knowing that peace *is* the only right answer.

Five Ways to Make Peace, Not War:

* Always respect others' beliefs, opinions, and actions, especially when different from your own.

* Hold the image of world peace in your heart and mind, feeling it every day.

* Detach yourself from the mob mentality and the single-minded point of view that the media creates.

* Choose the path of least resistance—walk away from arguments, fights, negative people, and explosive situations.

* Meditate or pray daily to create inner peace.

Think it. Say it. Feel it.

I am at peace with myself and the world.

My personal affirmations to make peace, not war:

....

....

....

....

....

29

Give to Others

MOST GIFTS ARE given out of guilt or obligation. We toss them back and forth for holidays or birthdays, like a grass-stained softball that's waiting to be caught by a person who feels it's rightfully theirs. Even charitable gifts can become more of a duty than an act of love. When I was growing up, my church dictated that 10 percent of the family's income should be donated to the church. When donations were low, church officials were quick to remind us of their rule by devoting an entire sermon to the subject. After that, people gave out of guilt *and* out of fear of being denied entrance at the gates of heaven!

Not all gifts need to come with attachments. In any given day, you can read about plenty of generous people giving to others. Some celebrities, who often have a lot to give, use their wealth and influence to create a better world for all of us. Many times, it is personal experience that leads them to a particular cause. Elizabeth Taylor's tireless support for an AIDS cure grew out of losing many fellow

actors and friends to the disease. Audrey Hepburn's malnutrition as a child during the Nazi occupation of Holland in World War II, as well as the medical and nutritional help UNICEF provided, became a catalyst for Hepburn's later role as a special ambassador to UNICEF, helping to improve conditions for hungry children in Africa and Latin America. A tour of an emergency shelter for abused children led actress Sela Ward to partner with Kentucky Fried Chicken's Colonel's Kids Program to buy and refurbish a twenty-five-acre children's home for abused and neglected children.

You don't have to be rich to give. Any gesture of generosity, no matter how small, makes a difference. True giving comes from the heart and can take many forms—money, gifts, love, compassion, physical assistance, time, food, services, advice, or even an open ear. When you give unconditionally, it's like releasing thousands of molecules of love and compassion into the universe; these attach themselves to people, places, and events. Remember, whatever you put out in this world comes back to you tenfold. It may not come back in the same form you sent it, but the universe will surely reciprocate, in some shape or form, in this lifetime or the next.

My friend Nanette is the queen of gift-giving, and it all comes from her heart. There isn't a holiday, occasion, event, or birthday that goes by without her making those moments special with her love, generosity, and presence. When I receive a gift from her, I can feel the love that surrounds it. It makes me happy and thankful. I feel that same love whenever I give a gift to someone, because that

person's happiness and gratitude are *my* gift. Giving *is* receiving, and receiving *is* giving. They are one and the same.

In the words of Audrey Hepburn, "Giving is like living. If you stop wanting to give . . . there's nothing more to live for." So, goddess, give freely and you will live happily.

Five Ways to Give to Others:

* Give someone a gift, just because.

* Give anonymously when appropriate.

* Never expect anything in return for your generosity.

* If you think someone could use some help, offer before she asks.

* Each morning, ask yourself how you can serve humanity—then do so.

Think it. Say it. Feel it.
I am open to share, give, and receive at any moment.

My personal affirmations to give to others:

....

....

....

....

30

Be Thankful

ONE OF THE first things I remember learning to say was "Thank you." It didn't matter how small the gift or deed, my mother would always say, "What do you say, Debbie?" The inevitable response, those two simple words, can be more beneficial to the psyche than years of therapy. Why? Because when you thank someone from your heart, you make that person feel appreciated, loved, and relevant. Isn't that what we all want out of life?

Sometimes it takes a tragedy to remind us to be grateful. After my mother's operation to remove a brain tumor, the doctors told us she would be home in six weeks. She subsequently spent three consecutive years in hospitals and nursing homes. Ironically, the anger and self-pity we felt in the first year were later replaced by gratitude. Years of hospital visits revealed countless families dealing with illnesses much worse than my mother's. We became thankful for our own fate, as bad as it seemed at the start. We also became grateful for life, particularly my mother's, since she lived another

ten years after her surgery. Even in the most difficult times, there's something for which to be thankful.

In her book *Simple Abundance Journal of Gratitude*, author Sarah Ban Breathnach writes, "Gratitude is the most passionate transformative force in the cosmos." She designed a daily journal where we can write what we're grateful for each day. She says, "If you give thanks for five gifts every day, in two months you may not look at your life in the same way as you might now."

Everything in life is a gift. Just think of the food you ate today. As small and insignificant as an apple may seem, there were many people involved in putting that apple on your table—the farmer who grew the tree, the worker who picked it, the trucker who transported it, the store owner who displayed it. Those are just a few people you can thank for that apple! And while you're at it, add Mother Nature to the mix—sunshine, rain, birds, insects, etc. They all played a part in that one little apple. How lucky you are to have all those forces joining together just for your personal nourishment.

How many times have you had an opportunity to thank someone or a higher power today . . . but didn't?

Five Ways to Be Thankful:

* No matter how bad a day you're having, think of one thing for which to be thankful.

* Say "Thank you" to people as often as possible . . . and mean it.

* Send "thank you" cards or notes after receiving dinners, gifts, parties, hospitality, advice, friendship, and business.

* Thank your children for being in your life and teach them the value of gratitude.

* Think of all those people who would trade their lives for yours in a second.

Think it. Say it. Feel it.

I am embraced by gratitude every day.

My personal affirmations to be thankful:

....

....

....

....

....

31

Believe

ONE OF MY all-time favorite movie lines comes from the 1947 version of *Miracle on 34th Street*. It was recited by both lead actors, John Payne and Maureen O'Hara: "Faith is believing in things when common sense tells you not to." There have been questions in my own life that I can only surrender to faith: "Am I really doing what I'm here for in life and work?" "Can I have a financially sustainable career doing what I love?" "Will I always have good health?" While some of my days are laced with tension, fear, and worry, I try to hang on to the faith that everything will turn out okay. I have no material evidence to support this belief; I just trust it.

I love watching TV biographies of famous women who were told early on in their careers that they wouldn't make it—and they did. For example, Sophia Loren was told that her features were too "big." Countless numbers of other women (famous or not) have been told they were not pretty enough or tall enough or smart enough or talented enough according to the "professionals" in their field or, even

worse, their own parents (the major influences in our lives). For the undaunted women profiled on TV, it's their faith in themselves and a higher power that keeps them going.

I believe that we are all spirits in earthly form and that there is a higher power or creator in whom I place my trust. But regardless of what your religious or spiritual beliefs are, or if you have any at all, you can still have faith. Faith is a trust that you place in custody or care of another. Even if you don't believe in anything beyond your own physical reality, you still have someone in whom to trust—yourself, the goddess. You cannot deny your own existence.

Early on in life, we learn to rely on skills and logic to make things happen. We set goals and believe that achieving them gives meaning to our lives—but somehow, even if we achieve all of our goals, we still have a hole in the "meaning" department because meaning isn't about achieving goals or controlling outcomes. It's about releasing control and expectation to faith. It's about believing that anything is possible and trusting the universe to make whatever should happen, happen at exactly the right time. Enough said. Enough thinking. Just release and believe.

Five Ways to Believe:

* Believe in miracles, especially those involving you.

* Regularly initiate conversations with goddesses, angels, fairies, your higher self, or any such spirit entities.

* Let go of attachment to our earthly definition of space and time.

* Imagine what it feels like to have a certain thing happen and keep that feeling for a minute each day.

* Use positive thoughts and words when envisioning the future.

Think it. Say it. Feel it.

I know what is true, even if I can't see it.

My personal affirmations to believe:

....

....

....

....

....

32

Simplify

Remember studying Maslow's hierarchy of human needs in high school? It seemed pretty simple. Once our basic needs—such as food, clothing, shelter, and security—are met, we start advancing up the pyramid to three more levels: social needs (love, entertainment, community), self-worth (ego satisfaction, recognition), and, finally, self-realization (personal/spiritual growth, contributing to mankind). Chances are, if you're an American woman, you're somewhere in the top three tiers of the pyramid, and if you're like most women, you're stuck in the gridlock between self-worth and self-realization (the ego doesn't like to be left behind). Our ego, which has the grip of a fierce undertow dragging us under the water, wave after wave, is one of the by-products of our rich American culture, where self-worth is often measured by the material things we have.

It's difficult to simplify our purchases when we succumb so easily to pressure from commercials, friends, and family: "What would

they all think if I don't have the latest, greatest, biggest?" It's important to distinguish between needs and wants; however, life would be no fun if you only bought what you needed. If you keep your purchases to 50 percent needs and 50 percent wants, you'll live a pretty modest life. If you slide the scale to 80/20, you'll simplify even more. Anything beyond that will probably have you living in a tree house!

Your home is a great place to simplify—not only when deciding on the size of it but also in choosing what's *inside*. My friend Jillian is an expert in feng shui, the ancient Chinese art of placement of items in your environment to maximize the flow of positive energy (chi). Although Jillian balances chi by adding certain things (crystals, plants, photos) to homes and offices, much of what she recommends to clients involves taking away items to reduce clutter and create more organized, cleaner spaces. The effects on your life can be remarkable. Once you simplify the environment in which you live or work, your life naturally flows more easily and happily. And why stop with material items? Perhaps there are people in your life who are cluttering your space as well. Do you really need them, or is it time to move on? Many women think they need a man in their life to be complete. If you're in a stressful relationship, think of how free you'll feel once you end it.

Freedom from any type of clutter in your life (whether it's human, animal, mineral, or your ego) opens up blocked areas. A simpler life allows you to use, appreciate, and enjoy everything you have, without the added stress of clutter but with more than enough space at any given time to add in the things and people that bring you

pleasure. That's when the goddess finally reaches the top of the pyramid: self-realization.

Five Ways to Simplify:

* Clean up your house clutter and donate what you don't want, need, or use.

* End relationships that aren't working anymore.

* Don't live on credit—only buy what you can truly afford.

* Trade money for time, and always choose time!

* Don't to be a slave to your mortgage.

Think it. Say it. Feel it.

My life is free of extraneous things, people, and thoughts.

My personal affirmations to simplify:

....

....

....

....

....

33

Give Up Guilt

We often associate innocence with young children—those who are pure and uncorrupted, blameless of any wrongdoing, incapable of feeling guilt. When we use the word "innocent" to describe an adult, however, its meaning changes to connote someone who is clueless, uninformed, ignorant, or unsophisticated. Why is that? Do only children have the right to be innocent? Today, even that right seems to be taken away as we rush our children into schools immediately after toilet training, expect them to speak like adults, compete in sports, excel in academics, and behave responsibly, as an adult would— all because these are the ways we define success in our society.

A friend of mine had to ask her teenage son to leave and live with his father because his behavior had become abusive and detrimental to her, his brother, and stepsiblings. He and his stepfather were constantly at each other's throats, causing more tension in an already volatile household. For the safety and sanity of everyone involved, it was best that he stayed a few miles away with his real father. Ever

since her son left, my friend's emotional and physical state has deteriorated as she agonizes daily about her decision and her guilt over making her son leave, even though she knows it's the best situation for all concerned, including herself. Society tells her that a "responsible" mother would not let her son go, and therefore she blames herself. There is another way she could choose to look at her decision. Her son is now with his father in a quiet, safe household. He is getting all the attention he needs, in addition to his own space and many privileges he did not have at home. He continues to go to the same school, and his mother is able to see him anytime. In addition, the tension in my friend's own home has been reduced. The siblings are getting along better, and my friend is not constantly playing referee between her current husband and her son. If she concentrated on all these benefits, she would not feel guilty.

The emphasis on being a responsible adult is sometimes highly overrated, while being carefree often gets a bum rap. The dictionary defines "carefree" as having "no worries or responsibilities." I'd rather define it as "freeing your worries from your mind." If responsibility results in guilt over things you can't or shouldn't change, then you *are* being irresponsible—to yourself. Guilt is an unnecessary burden on your life; it's akin to carrying around a second head on your shoulders, a head that devours all your positive energy. Leaving guilt behind lightens your heart and soul. It allows you to live in the present and move forward in life. It allows your true goodness to shine brightly, without being hidden behind a veil of darkness.

Innocence is a goddess's natural state. It is the state in which you are born. (Clearly, I don't believe in the original sin theory.) It is you without the burden of guilt about things you said or didn't say, did or didn't do. (Women seem to worry a lot about that stuff.) I don't believe any higher power ever intended us to have such man-made, manufactured guilt that lingers on and on. Remorse for a wrongdoing, maybe, but even that is meant to be followed by self-forgiveness, so that we can move on with our lives.

Being innocent is not ignorant. It is knowing all there is to know at this very moment.

Five Ways to Give Up Guilt:

* Keep your thoughts and actions focused on the present moment.

* Bury your regrets; nothing can change the past.

* Have a conversation with a three-year-old.

* Don't do or say anything out of guilt.

* Forgive and forget at all times.

Think it. Say it. Feel it.

I happily release all attachment to guilt or regret.

My personal affirmations to give up guilt:

....

....

....

....

....

34

Fill Your Foundation

WE ALL GROW up with a set of experiences and lessons that shape our value system and create our foundation in life. In housing construction, the stuff that holds the foundation together is called mortar. In life, that mortar is called integrity. Like the foundations of houses, foundations in life can either start with cracks or develop them later.

Even if you grow up in the perfect Beaver Cleaver household, things happen in life that cause stress on your foundation. Like a house settling as a result of gravity and bad weather, your life develops cracks as a result of difficult situations—divorce, neglect, fear, abuse, peer pressure, work stress, illness. On the other hand, the seemingly most fortunate life circumstances can also crack a foundation. You wonder how people who look like they have it all (money, fame, and stardom) can resort to damaging or ending their lives, but that's not an unusual backdrop for the story line of many

famous people's biographies. Women like Janis Joplin, Marilyn Monroe, and even Martha Stewart have gotten caught in a tangled web of mistakes.

Saranne Rothberg is a woman who decided to fill her cancer-induced cracks with laughter. She started a nonprofit organization called Comedy Cures, which helps people in tough situations laugh. Her traveling Laugh-A-Thons visit all kinds of groups around the country, from hospital patients to the surviving families of 9/11 victims. Five years after her fatal diagnosis, Saranne has no signs of the disease.

I often sign notes and letters with the words "Love, Light, and Laughter." "Love" and "laughter" for obvious reasons, many of which are repeated in this book. "Light "is a reminder to always gravitate toward all things bright, positive, and cheery in life and then to shine your own inner goddess light with so much intensity that that it cuts through and dissipates any darkness around you. If you fill your life with those three L's, you will always act with integrity and joy and be able to break whatever negative patterns you may have been exposed to, or continue to hold on to, in your life. While you can't change the foundation created by the environment in which you grew up, or the subsequent life events that follow, you do have the power to fill in the cracks that may form with positive things like love, light, and laughter.

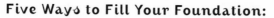

Five Ways to Fill Your Foundation:

* Always tell the truth.

* If you feel like you're in a rut, use the three L's (love, light, and laughter) to help you out.

* Honor your body with good nutrition and exercise — avoid recreational drugs.

* Never compromise your integrity — stand your ground.

* Don't keep anything that isn't yours, even praise.

Think it. Say it. Feel it.
I have everything I need to be complete and to live my life with integrity.

My personal affirmations to fill my foundation:

....

....

....

....

....

35

Have Patience

Watching mothers and their children interact provides great examples of patience or impatience. Not having children myself, I'm sometimes in awe at the incredible amount of patience that mothers can have (without causing any physical harm to the child). I commend my sister, Angela, for trying to teach her daughter, Sydney, about patience at a very early age. When Sydney was about two years old, she entered that demanding two-year-old phase, where she wanted what she wanted when she wanted it, and that was NOW! Angela would calmly tell her that she had to be patient. Then she would ask Sydney if she knew what patience meant. Sydney would reply, "No," and Angela would explain that patience meant to wait a minute. After awhile, Sydney started to remember the answer, and when Angela said, "You need to be patient. Do you know what patience means?," Sydney would reply, "It means wait a minute." After that, if she stopped whining for awhile, she would

get rewarded. This became a little game that gave my niece the attention she wanted while also teaching her something.

We often go through life like a two-year-old child—not willing to wait for anything, whether it's as trivial as our turn in line at the supermarket or as serious as our lifelong dream. How many of you get frustrated when the driver in front of you is just going the speed limit? When you have to listen to a girlfriend who tells long, boring stories all the time? When you need to save money before buying something? While we all strive for instant gratification (hence our huge credit card debt), if we were willing to wait a little instead of pushing all the time, our lives would be less frustrating and more contented.

Sometimes it feels as though we're wasting time doing nothing when, in reality, much is happening. There's a card in the Osho tarot deck that has no picture on it—it's completely black with one word: "No-Thingness." You might think its meaning is negative; however, it is quite inspiring. It addresses the fear we have when nothing is happening, but that is precisely when something is about to be born. It is the time when all is possible. It is the journey in between "things." I have a friend who launched a line of inspiring home products. She worked hard on all the ideas and tried selling them to many retail outlets, but only a few smaller stores bought them, and the products didn't sell quickly. Instead of continuing to call more retailers, she waited. And during the time she was waiting, she came up with an even more clever package for her products.

The new package received a much better reception and allowed her to start fresh with new retailers that otherwise might not have considered her had they had an unfavorable sales experience with the original packages.

Usually events happen in life at exactly the right time, which may not be when you would like them to happen. Have you ever thought that those extra five minutes at the automatic teller machine, waiting behind someone who seemingly can't read or push buttons faster than a toddler, might save you from being at an intersection just at the moment when someone decides to run a red light? Next time your patience is tested, be a goddess in waiting—it could turn out to be a blessing.

Five Ways to Have Patience:

* Daydream about pleasant places or memories whenever you're waiting in line.

* Send loving thoughts to anyone trying your patience.

* Listen and evaluate a situation before you speak or act.

* Don't look at the clock every five minutes.

* Be thankful for a delay; it could save your life and/or create an opportunity.

Think it. Say it. Feel it.

I have patience, knowing that everything happens in perfect timing.

My personal affirmations to have patience:

....

....

....

....

....

36

Love, Love, Love

HAVE YOU EVER asked yourself, "Why am I here?" This is the question that has excited and bedeviled the minds of historians, theologians, and the entire human race since the beginning of time. Often we're looking for a very complicated, deep, and mysterious answer, but after we peel away all the layers of social conditioning, peer pressure, religious dogma, and media images that we've been exposed to since birth, the answer becomes quite simple. It's LOVE! We're here to learn to give and receive love—unconditionally.

Mother Teresa said, "We can do no great things—only small things with great love." There are many ways to show or feel love in life. For example, in my home growing up, love was expressed through food. My Italian parents had a hard time saying the words, "I love you," but I still felt loved in the way I was nurtured and comforted with delicious food. Even as an adult, when I came home to visit, my mother always managed to have my favorite meal ready for me, despite the fact that she had become disabled. I knew how

much effort it took for her to make that tray of eggplant parmesan, and I truly appreciated and enjoyed every bite of it!

With the plethora of self-help books and tapes available, we've all heard the expression "You must first learn to love yourself before you can love others." While most women aren't ready to stand naked in front of a mirror admiring themselves like Aphrodite, the Greek goddess of love and beauty, it's important to start somewhere (maybe an earlobe), so that you can begin to love not only your physical attributes but everything about you. The way you talk, act, and feel—imperfections and all. Self-love also means forgiving yourself for any misdeeds or harmful thoughts.

Once you start the process of loving yourself, you open the door of reverence and love for all life—people, animal, plants, situations, nations, earth. You choose to replace hate and anger with love, because you know that harming another (emotionally or physically) is incongruent with life. Even if someone has harmed you, love allows you to forgive that person. There are true stories of people who have forgiven their attackers, sacrificed their lives for the safety of others, given when they had nothing to give, or helped a stranger in need. All of these are acts of unconditional love.

Your collective thoughts, words, actions, and emotions create the environment in which you live. If you choose love over hate, love is what you will bring into your life and into the world. You'll feel good about yourself and others and you'll live a happier, more peaceful and meaningful life, knowing that love is *all there is*.

There is no power in the universe greater than the power of love.

Five Ways to Love, Love, Love:

* Find something, no matter how small, to love about yourself and remind yourself of it every day. Build this list with time.

* Send loving thoughts to all people or situations you dislike.

* Consider yourself and all human beings to be the children of the Goddess—perfect in every way, no matter how we outwardly appear to be.

* Never harm anyone—emotionally or physically.

* Extend all of the above to the animal and plant kingdom, and remember to be thankful for those that you consume.

Think it. Say it. Feel it.
I love myself and my life.

My personal affirmations to love, love, love:

....

....

....

....

....

37

Stop Chasing Perfection

DON'T YOU WANT the perfect life? The perfect job, mate, family, home? There's nothing wrong with that desire if you define perfection on your *own* terms. Usually we let others (a friend, teacher, parents, and the media) define it for us, and then we spend the rest of our lives trying to live someone else's fantasy.

Women, in particular, are bombarded with hundreds of images of perfection on a daily basis, all of which promise happiness, yet few of which real women can achieve. (In a magazine interview, Jane Fonda said, "Most women—no matter how beautiful—grow up feeling their bodies are not perfect.") Magazine photos of even the plus-size models don't dare show one little dimple of cellulite on their size 14 thighs! TV celebrity chefs demonstrate how to cook the perfect gourmet meal in minutes, and design experts tell us how to serve it up on perfectly decorated tables. This is not real life for most of us. Have you ever had the time, energy, or desire

to decoupage your own napkin rings? How about pressing your own olives for the bread dip at your next dinner party? Just thinking about it makes me exhausted and begs the question: why?

There was a time when I wouldn't invite guests to my house unless it was thoroughly scrubbed by professional cleaners a day or two beforehand—as if someone would really notice the dust bunny lurking on the floor behind the toilet. Surely it would spoil their evening and any image of perfection they'd conceived about me.

The unending quest for perfection over the course of a lifetime ends up looking like a horrible makeup job that smothers reality in layers of noticeably thick cover-up, mismatched colors, and empty promises. If you think you must be perfect, nothing will ever make you feel perfect *enough*—unless you want to sell your soul and become a Stepford wife. Do you want your kids to remember how clean you kept the house or how many fun things you did together? I'm not saying you shouldn't keep your house neat, work hard to be promoted, improve your tennis skills, or even get that nose job you've always wanted. Just make sure you're doing all of it for yourself, not to meet someone else's definition of perfection. Your imperfections are what make you unique, vulnerable, and loving—those are the qualities in life worth pursuing.

Chase the things in life that make you truly happy. Being a happy goddess will always outrank being a perfect goddess.

Five Ways to Stop Chasing Perfection:

* Make a list of all your unique qualities and assign a positive word to each of them.

* Remind yourself that what you see in magazines and on TV isn't REAL—it's merely entertainment.

* Adjust your expectations of yourself and others based on each individual's ability and interest.

* Shine in those areas that come naturally to you and don't worry about the rest.

* Ask yourself if going the extra mile matters and why.

Think it. Say it. Feel it.
I am uniquely perfect in many ways by my own definition.

My personal affirmations to stop chasing perfection:

....

....

....

....

....

38

Touch Somebody

Remember your first crush and how the slightest brush of his shoulder (or her shoulder, if you prefer women) on yours would make your racing, pounding heart feel like it was going to break through your body at any second? That's the power of touch. There is plenty of research confirming the benefits of touch—studies show that babies who are held more become better adjusted and happier in life, and that people instantly feel better with just a simple hug. A well-meaning, loving embrace immediately creates a positive emotional response by balancing energy and calming nerves. Imagine what a full-body massage does! (I don't know of any woman who doesn't love the feeling of being stroked by her mate or by a professional massage therapist.)

The human touch can have a profound and comforting effect on people who are ill or dying, and yet these are the people whom we often refuse, or forget, to touch. Let's face it, we don't all feel called to wash the sores off starving children in Calcutta as Mother

Teresa did, or to hug diseased children in southern Sudan as Audrey Hepburn did. It's natural to be uncomfortable around someone who is suffering and to resist touching people when illness has ravaged their bodies. But when you love someone, you can push yourself beyond her physical appearance and connect with the person underneath—the person who desperately needs to feel that she's still a part of this world, still loved, still wanted, still alive.

In the book *The Power of Patience*, author M. J. Ryan talks about her adopted Chinese daughter, Ana, who used to wake every night in a hysterical state. During those episodes, all M. J. could do was hold Ana and tell her she was safe until she fell back asleep. After almost four years, the night terrors finally stopped.

When my aunt was dying of breast cancer, her body was burned and bloated from chemotherapy and radiation. I visited her often and sat on her bed, just close enough to chat but not to touch. Then one day, she asked me to rub lotion all over her. I knew I didn't feel comfortable running my hands along the scabs and bruises on her skin, but I gladly obliged, as I was happy to be able to do anything that made her feel better. I'm not sure I would have thought of it on my own, but she only had to ask me once. After that, each time I saw her, I went straight for the lotion.

Touch, with good intentions, can be healing, comforting, pleasurable, or erotic, all of which are imperative for goddesses and their partners. Often, couples who are together for many years only touch each other during sex, but it's so important to remember to stay connected via touch during everyday life—a delicate kiss when you

leave or return home, a neck massage while one of you is stuck in front of the computer doing work, or a warm embrace on a cold evening out. I'll take all of the above!

Five Ways to Touch Somebody:

* Hug and kiss your children, not only when they're babies but also as they mature.

* Look beyond what you see in those who are sick and touch them; they need physical connection to survive.

* Embrace a person in sadness, if they're amenable to it.

* Indulge in therapeutic body treatments and massage.

* Hold hands with your partner.

Think it. Say it. Feel it.
I am open to feel with my heart and my hands.

My personal affirmations to touch somebody:

....
....
....
....
....

39

Don't Compare

I DON'T KNOW OF any woman (heterosexual or lesbian) who doesn't check out other women—sometimes to admire but mostly to compare: "Why can't my thighs be that slim!" "Thank God my hair is not that frizzy!" It's natural to compare. Kids compare toys. Parents compare children. Teachers compare students. Men compare . . . let's not go there! Even women who are considered icons of beauty compare themselves to other women and find faults in their own appearances. In a magazine interview, Raquel Welch, who wanted to be a dancer, said she thought she should be shorter and more muscular, like the girls in her ballet class. Farrah Fawcett, on the other hand, thought her legs were too muscular as compared with other beauties of her time.

Every woman compares what she has in life (from looks to wealth and everything in between) to what other people have. These comparisons tend to create a breeding ground for negative emotions

like jealousy, resentment, inadequacy, and even anger—not the kind of feelings you want in your basket of personality traits.

There was a time (when I was writing my first book) when I was jealous of writers with agents. I learned everything I could on how to find agents, how to approach them, how to do a book proposal, etc. I was sure I would get a great agent. Months went by, and the rejection letters continued to pour in. Each time I met an author who had an agent, I hated myself for being jealous. When that book was finished, I decided to self-publish. I don't know why I didn't get an agent, but I finally accepted that finding an agent wasn't meant to happen for me at that particular time. Maybe with an agent, my book wouldn't have been published. Maybe it would have been out of print by now. Maybe I would've signed with the wrong person. What initially seemed like the one thing I wanted (because other authors had it) might not have been the best thing for my future publishing career.

Comparisons create an insatiable hunger in your life. There will always be someone you perceive to be in a better position than you, whether that person has a new car, a smaller nose, or a more loving partner. And there will also always be someone in a worse position than you. Whenever you're feeling cheated in life, think of all those people who would love to have your life. It's like getting on the end of a really long line in a department store and wishing you could exchange places with the woman up front—a few minutes later, you look around and see ten more people standing behind you. All of a sudden, you're happy with your place in line.

Unlike checkout lines, life doesn't have a first and last. Each of us has a unique place in life and a role to play. How you look or what you have is not about being better or worse. Those are external characteristics that can change in an instant. You *can* better your life or strive to be a better human being, but that striving comes from within—from a love of your own life and that of others. It is not attached to your zip code, clothing, car, or body.

Five Ways to Not Compare:

* Be grateful for the gift of waking up each morning and being alive.

* Remember that we each have a different path in life that we've chosen.

* If you must compare to feel good, compare down instead of up (that is, compare yourself to those who must live with less than you do).

* Live within your means and be proud of having limited debt.

* Focus on your own life and goals without comparing them to someone else's.

Think it. Say it. Feel it.

I cherish and own my life, which is uniquely mine.

My personal affirmations to not compare:

....

....

....

....

....

40

Move with the Flow

IN AN EDITORIAL for her magazine, Oprah Winfrey spoke about the importance of finding the flow in life and following it. She recalled an interview she had early in her career with Robin Williams —clearly not the most sedate person to pin down in a standard Q & A format. But once she allowed herself to go with the flow of Robin's animated and erratic persona, all was fine. Oprah has since trusted the natural rhythm of life, knowing that whatever happens, she'll be okay.

When my family was hit with tragic illness, all I wanted was my perfect life back. Before the hospitals and nursing homes. Before the battles with doctors and insurance companies. Before the rancid smell of sickness and grinding noises of life support. After awhile, I realized that I had three choices. I could live in the past and be angry over the events that had fallen upon my family. I could live in the future and worry about what terrible thing could

happen next. Or I could adapt to my new life and accept each day as it came. I had no control over these changes that leapt into my life, including the four family deaths that followed. However, I did have control over whether I chose to embrace them or not—which made them a part of my life, not something that was happening outside of it.

No day is exactly like another. Women are constantly challenged to adjust in a changing environment. Some of those changes are small, and we manage them without a thought—a daughter's delayed ballet practice, a sudden head cold, a picnic planned on a rainy day. Some are huge—a death, a marriage, a move. Either way, they are all just moments. Moments that dissolve into new moments. Nothing is permanent. Your house, your car, your jewelry, and your money are merely props given to you to help you navigate through life. These, too, shall pass. You don't know when. It could take a lifetime or just a day, but once you accept the impermanence of life, you also accept that anything can vanish in a moment, including your own life.

It's impossible to prepare for unexpected changes, but when they come (and they will), you should welcome and continue to learn from them. Regardless of whether these changes are joyful, frustrating, or devastating, they will always advance you to another step on your life's path. Thankfully, life continues to happen. If you can adapt with it, your journey as a goddess will be much happier.

Five Ways to Move with the Flow:

* Live in the present moment; it's the only place you can effect change.

* When something bad happens, ask yourself what you can learn from it.

* Accept that any plan you make may change.

* Be open-minded about others' attitudes, opinions, and ways of doing things.

* Don't try to control everything that happens in life— you can't.

Think it. Say it. Feel it.

I easily adapt to all changes that occur in my life, day by day.

My personal affirmations to move with the flow:

....

....

....

....

....

41

Slow Down

LIFE IS ONE big fat rush. We want fast food to eat quickly, fast cars to get us there sooner, fast sex to fit our busy schedule, fast money to spend freely, and fast gadgets to do double the work in half the time. And, yes . . . I know you want to get to the end of this essay as fast as possible! We're driving our lives at ninety miles per hour on a path meant for walking.

You can accomplish a lot in the fast lane, but rarely do you enjoy yourself, and what happens when you hit that inevitable hairpin turn? You frantically try to decelerate, veer to the right, and stay calm while you're about to collide with an oncoming car, all while screaming, "#@%@#! Where did this come from?" Sound familiar? But if you weren't going so fast, you might have been able to avoid the accident; or maybe you would have noticed the warning signs a mile back. Life's curves give us two choices: slow down or break down. Don't wait for something terrible to happen to shift your life into a lower gear. If you've forgotten how, just spend an hour or two with a child.

A few years ago, I took my friend Gina's four-year-old daughter, Chelsea, out for the afternoon. Of course, I had a plan for the day that started with lunch out followed by games at home. I allotted about an hour for lunch. Okay, I can hear you mothers giggling right about now. A four-year-old. A plan. An hour. Good luck!

From the second our visit began, I realized we'd probably be a *bit* off schedule. Maybe it was the ten-minute seatbelt-buckling exercise, which Chelsea wanted to do herself. Or perhaps the fifteen-minute leisurely stroll from the car to the restaurant . . . two blocks away. When we sat down and began a long discussion about plain cheese pizza versus pepperoni, I started to relax into Chelsea's pace. No doubt my favorite subject—food—had something to do with it. After lunch, we walked to an ice cream parlor half a block away. I don't know how long that took; I had forgotten about time by then. Chelsea ordered bubble-gum ice cream, and after I gobbled up my mint chip in about a minute, I watched in fascination as she alternated among eating the ice cream, chewing the gum, and cleaning her mouth. Four hours later, we arrived back home. We didn't have time to play the games I planned, but it didn't matter. We had a delightful afternoon. Once I slowed down, I was able to enjoy Chelsea's company while giving my mind a much-needed break.

Weeks later, when Gina heard that Chelsea had ordered that bubble-gum ice cream, we both had a good laugh as she said, "Oh, no . . . I should have warned you about that! It takes her forever to eat." Better that I didn't know; I might've missed all the fun.

Next time you're tempted to rush, think of the most beautiful

goddess you know walking (notice I didn't say "running") the face of the earth. I'm sure you couldn't imagine this woman rushing anything. Close your eyes, take a deep breath, and become her: calm, knowing, and relaxed.

Five Ways to Slow Down:

* Do the speed limit—listen to music or books in traffic.

* Replace a "to do" item that's not about life and death (they never are) with time for yourself . . . alone.

* Eat slower—sit down, chew, savor each bite, no TV.

* Under-schedule every day (especially your children's activities), and let life happen in between commitments.

* Do something with a child (play a game, take a walk).

> **Think it. Say it. Feel it.**
> *I live my life at a comfortable pace with plenty of downtime.*

My personal affirmations to slow down:

....

....

....

....

....

42

Accept Your Life

I T'S SO EASY TO ACCEPT the good stuff when it happens to us. We savor those fortunate moments like a rich, slow-melting piece of Godiva chocolate caressing our tongues. (I don't know of any goddess who wouldn't enjoy that!) But when we're faced with bad news or unpleasant feelings, we fight, ignore, or deny them like the plague. We dig in our heels and think, "Not in my lifetime is this going to happen!"

Now, I'm not suggesting that you roll over and play dead when life deals you a bad set of cards. You should always attempt to change and improve whatever you can, but sometimes a tornado sweeps into your life without cause or warning. While you can't prevent it, you can certainly live through it. That means acknowledging it and adjusting your life to accommodate and embrace it—without anger or guilt. Major setbacks—no life comes without them—are often lessons that help you change your life for the better.

When Suzanne Somers was told she had breast cancer, she

refused to be a victim. Just as she had done with the myriad other challenges in her life (an abusive, alcoholic father; teen pregnancy; single motherhood; and a scandalous career episode, to name a few), she accepted the illness as another learning experience; however, she immediately put the wheels in motion to heal herself. In her book *The Sexy Years*, she says cancer taught her that she was surrounded by love and could overcome any obstacle in life. She also learned to appreciate and enjoy the best moments of each day.

By accepting the direction your life takes, whether within or outside of your control, you accept life itself. You become more tolerant of others and more content with your personal situation, whatever it may be at the time. You realize that every event in your life—trivial or life changing, fortuitous or tragic—eventually comes to an end. Nothing ever stays the same. How boring and hopeless it would be if it did.

Life will always be a series of ups and downs. For some women, it's a roller coaster ride. For others, it's just a few bumps on a rather flat road. Either way, you'll be happier if you hold on, pay attention, and embrace every bit of the ride.

Five Ways to Accept Your Life:

* Say and believe each morning that you are open to whatever the day brings.

* Consider the death of a loved one a natural part of life— talk about it, work through it.

* Remember that unhappy events and emotions are temporary—don't deny them, or they'll come back to haunt you.

* Embrace misfortune; it will make the good times feel that much better.

* Don't worry or blame yourself for things out of your control—go with the flow.

> ### Think it. Say it. Feel it.
> *I welcome and embrace any outcome of my day and my life.*

My personal affirmations to accept my life:

....

....

....

....

....

43

Respect Yourself

MUCH OF A woman's self-worth is influenced early on by her parents, particularly her mother. Some of us can spend our entire lives (and many hours in therapy) trying to figure out why we can't be the person our mothers want us to be. Later on in life, other family members, friends, colleagues, and bosses may also have unpleasant opinions of us. We store all of these criticisms in one "unworthy self" basket, like a bunch of rotten eggs. Some of us never regain our self-worth. Yes, *regain*. We begin life with a storehouse of personal power and self-worth. As babies, we demand that respect and attention. We kick and scream until we get it! But somewhere along the line, through all of our social conditioning, we forget it's there. We forget how special a goddess each one of us is. We forget to listen to our inner voices and tap into our power. We forget to throw away those rotten opinions and collect only the good eggs.

There will *always* be people who are critical of you. It's a way for

them to exercise control, much like the alpha dog in the pack, who maintains her status by constantly reminding you that you're the runt of the litter. So, where does a goddess get R-E-S-P-E-C-T? You have to find out what respect means to YOU! And that entails looking in the mirror and respecting yourself for who you are. If you are a human being, you *are* something, and hence you must have value. You're the only one who can assign what that value is.

Sometimes it takes others to help us see that value. Supermodel Iman grew up with low self-esteem and had no date to her prom. Even when a famous photographer asked her to pose for him, she still felt insecure about her looks, especially her lengthy neck. Her success in modeling helped her appreciate and honor her exotic look. She now runs her own cosmetics company for women of color.

You don't respect yourself if you fill your mind with self-deprecating thoughts every day. You don't respect yourself if you stay in an abusive relationship. You don't respect yourself if you damage your body with drugs, alcohol, or excessive eating. Drew Barrymore was once a child actress headed for a tragic burnout. Her addiction to drugs and alcohol started at age eleven, with a suicide attempt a few years later. However, by age fifteen, after months of rehab, she was able to conquer her addictions and start a new life. Having spent most of her teen years looking outside of herself for love or approval, today she considers her best friend to be none other than herself. From self-abuse to self-love, Drew has emerged as a confident and compassionate young woman. In a *People* magazine interview, when

discussing the geeky, awkward character she played in the movie *Never Been Kissed*, Drew said, "I wanted to talk about, for one, feeling good about who you are and naturally embracing that. A person's looks are never going to make you love them or like them." Today, Drew lives her life with compassion and generosity. She is known to treat everyone who works for her with equal kindness, and she has become a philanthropist who dedicates much of her time and resources to charities that support women and animals.

Look in the mirror. Honor the goddess you see both inside and out, from the color of your skin and the shape of your body to the love in your heart and the heart of your soul. Love yourself. Believe in yourself. Know that you a perfect being, deserving of respect from both yourself and from others.

Five Ways to Respect Yourself:

* Tell someone if a comment she's made to you makes you feel inadequate or unworthy.

* Treat yourself to something special (massage, dessert, vacation) to acknowledge a personal or professional accomplishment.

* Throw a party to celebrate a milestone in your life (birthday, promotion, divorce).

* Don't succumb to other people's expectations of who you should be or what you should do.

* Praise and compliment your family, friends, and colleagues—like a reflection in a mirror, it'll naturally increase your own self-worth.

Think it. Say it. Feel it.

I honor and appreciate my body, mind, and spirit.

My personal affirmations to respect myself:

....

....

....

....

....

44

Trust Your Inner Voice

Scientists say we use less than 10 percent of our brains. As minute as that sounds, 10 percent is enough to run all of our bodily functions, from our reflexes to blood circulation to breathing. In addition, it's enough to learn anything, from how to read to how we can fly to the moon and back.

We're used to exercising the part of the brain that teaches us rational thinking; however, if we grew up in a different time and culture, such as Native American culture hundreds of years before the first Europeans arrived, we would have placed equal emphasis on exercising the intuitive side of our brain—our psychic ability that connects us with nature, animals, and spirit. Imagine if you kept a child from standing up and walking in the first couple years of her life. As is the case when any muscle isn't used, atrophy would quickly set in: her leg muscles would be underdeveloped, her ankles would be weak, and her spinal vertebrae would be compacted. If you tried

to stand the child up at any age thereafter, she would topple over. That's what happens to our intuitive abilities when we don't develop them.

Intuition is receiving information without a rational thinking process. Receptive and communicative qualities are most often associated with women—you've never heard the term "men's intuition," have you? Over the course of history, those once-revered feminine qualities have been forgotten or forbidden by the people in charge (mainly men), who were intimidated or threatened by these extraordinary powers. Even in today's more liberal society, these abilities are sometimes lumped into the same category as articles in the supermarket tabloids about women giving birth to turtles!

Whether you know or accept it on a conscious level or not, your intuition is constantly at work. It helps you make big decisions in life, warns you of danger, and brings you guidance from the spirit world. After the 1989 earthquake in northern California, during which a portion of the Bay Bridge collapsed, I heard many stories of people who were supposed to be on that bridge at that time but weren't, because of strange coincidences or seemingly trivial decisions they made that sent them in another direction. They weren't meant to die on the bridge that day, and their intuition knew it.

Sophia is the ancient goddess of female wisdom. She is known and revered by Christians, Jews, Gnostics, and Pagans alike for being the mother of all things (including creation). Think of Sophia as your inner voice—your own personal GPS system for your life.

She contains the complete itinerary for your trip here on earth, which your conscious mind (remember that 10 percent) quickly forgets after birth. Every once in awhile, you tap into that remaining 90 percent and hear her (your inner voice) saying things like "Go this way," "Take that job," and "Stay away from that man." She speaks to you in between the chatter of your day and during your dreams at night, to keep you on track with your life plan. Your inner voice is a powerful tool that helps you navigate the winding road of life. Tune in and listen wisely.

Five Ways to Trust Your Inner Voice:

* Keep a notepad and pen by your bed and record your dreams as soon as you wake from them—interpret them in the morning.

* Honor your hunches even if your rational mind is singing another tune.

* Meditate on a regular basis.

* Ask spirit for guidance with difficult decisions.

* Every day, ask your inner voice to help you stay on track with your life plan.

Think it. Say it. Feel it.

I am open to receiving and acting upon information from my spirit every day.

My personal affirmations to trust my inner voice:

....

....

....

....

....

"Happiness is like a butterfly:
the more you chase it, the more it
will elude you, but if you turn your attention
to other things, it will come
and sit softly on your shoulder . . ."

—THOREAU

Acknowledgments

To Karen Bouris and the team at Inner Ocean Publishing, thank you for your excitement, support, and professionalism. Karen, I admire your quest to empower women, and I'm right there beside you. John, thanks for publishing inspiring books in one of the most inspiring places on earth! Mark, thanks for introducing me to Inner Ocean and for your sales and marketing savvy. Heather, thanks for your invaluable editorial direction—I loved the process! Katie, thanks for being an awesome marketeer and publicist. Alma, thanks for your wonderful ideas and for keeping it all moving.

Joe, you've lived through it all with me—the highest of highs and lowest of lows—and you're still the best husband and friend a goddess could have. Thank you for all your encouragement, unconditional love, humor, positive outlook, and faith in me. I love you, and I'm sure I've loved you for many lifetimes. I'm so happy to have you on this journey with me.

To Angela, my sister, you have always believed in me and been proud of me, ever since we were little girls. Thanks for being there all my life. Thank you for all your love, advice, ideas, proofreading, and your great sense of comic timing! I can't imagine our lives without all those bursts of uncontrollable laughter together.

Jillian Auberger, thank you for being an extraordinary friend—the first person I call whenever something happens (good or bad). Thanks

for helping me launch this book idea with a beautiful prototype and many loving words of support.

Susan D'Elia, thank you for always putting me up on a pedestal when, in fact, you deserve the accolades! Thanks for your friendship and your keen set of editing eyes in the early essays of this book.

To all my goddess girlfriends, especially Kimberly Drake, Nanette Saab, Jenai Lane, Gina Reidy, Jeannine Klopocki, Lisa Gebbia, and Susan Grima, thank you for many glorious years of friendship, love, and laughter, as well as your support and input for this book!

And to Simone, Jackie Haller, and all the goddesses of Wednesday night meditation, thank you for being beacons of light.

About the Author

Debbie Gisonni is the Goddess of Happiness™, and founder of Real Life Lessons®, a company dedicated to personal well-being, spiritual growth, and business success. Through various media, she makes life happier and easier for women by helping them connect their sometimes forgotten inner power with the real life issues they face every day—from the tragic to the trivial.

Debbie is also a freelance writer, columnist for iVillage.com, and the author of *Vita's Will: Real Life Lessons about Life, Death & Moving On*. She has been a guest on numerous radio and TV shows across the United States and is an experienced speaker who has addressed audiences of all kinds.

Originally from the Bronx, New York, Debbie now lives on the West Coast with her two biggest passions in life—her husband and dogs. Other passions include cooking and entertaining, physical fitness, clothing and shoes, painting, interior design feng shui, tarot, dancing, all kinds of music, and laughter.

Contact: www.reallifelessons.com
Send mail to: debbieg@reallifelessons.com or
Real Life Lessons
PMB # 396, 1017 El Camino Real
Redwood City, CA 94063-1632